Buyer's Price Guide

CONTINENTAL PORCELAIN

by

Judith H. Miller, M.A.

Consultant Editor

Gordon Lang, Sotheby's

mJm

PUBLICATIONS
Pugin's Hall
Finchden Manor
Tenterden
Kent
telephone 058 06 2234

Reprographic illustration work by
G.H. Graphics, St. Leonards-on-Sea, East Sussex

Photosetting by Ardek Photosetters
(division of Mainline Typesetters Ltd.)
Warrior Square Station Forecourt
St. Leonards-on-Sea, East Sussex

Made and printed in Great Britain by
Robert MacLehose, Scotland

The Publishers would like to acknowledge the great assistance given by:

Aldridges, 130-132 Walcot Street, Bath, Avon.

Anderson and Garland, Market Street, Newcastle-upon-Tyne NE1 6XA.

Bonhams, Montpelier Street, London, S.W.7.

Christie, Manson & Woods Ltd., 8 King Street, London SW17 6QT.

Christie, Manson & Woods International Inc., 502 Park Avenue, New York 10022.

Christie's East, 219 East 67th Street, New York 10021.

Christie's (International) S.A., 8 Place de la Taconnerie, 1204 Geneva.

Crispin Antiques, 10 The Broadway, Amersham, Bucks.

Dacre Son and Hartley, 1-5 The Grove, Ilkley, Yorkshire.

Geering & Colyer, Hawkhurst, Kent.

Henry Spencer & Sons, 20 The Square, Retford, Notts.

Langlois, 10 Waterloo Street, Jersey, C.I.

Louis Taylor & Sons, Percy Street, Hanley, Stoke-on-Trent.

Market Bosworth Antiques, Market Bosworth, Nuneaton, Warwickshire.

Melvyn Traub, 148-149 Grays Antique Market, 58 Davies Street, London W.1.

Morphets of Harrogate, The Mart, 4 & 6 Albert Street, Harrogate, Yorks.

Neales of Nottingham, 192 Mansfield Road, Nottingham.

Peter Wilson, Market Street, Nantwich, Cheshire.

Phillips Auctioneers, Blenstock House, 7 Blenheim Street, London W1Y 0AS.

Sotheby Bearne, Rainbow, Torquay TQ2 5TG.

Sotheby Belgravia, 19 Motcomb Street, London SW1X 8LB.

Sotheby Beresford Adams, Booth Mansion, 28 Watergate Street, Chester CH1 1NP.

Sotheby King & Chasemore, Station Road, Pulborough, West Sussex RH20 1AJ.

Sotheby, Parke Bernet and Co., 34-35 New Bond Street, London W1A 2AA.

Sotheby Park Bernet Monaco S.A., P.O. Box 45, Sporting d'Hiver, Place du Casino, Monaco.

CONTENTS

PREFACE

This book is intended purely as a guide to the products of the principal European porcelain factories of the eighteenth and nineteenth centuries. It is by no means exhaustive, but by careful selection of almost 500 illustrations, it provides a comprehensive picture of the styles and scope of some 45 different factories whose products are to be found in shops, galleries and auction rooms.

For convenience, entries are arranged in alphabetical order by factory name, and then again by alphabetical arrangement of groups of objects within the factory entry. Thus, the Meissen factory, for example may be located by means of the contents list or the headlines on each page, where its products will be found to run from 'barrels' to 'vases'. Individual items, decorators, etc. will be located best by means of the index.

Every entry has, in addition to its attribution and description, an indication of the price range within which the accompanying object would be likely to be bought on the open market. Naturally, these cannot be taken as absolute judgements of the worth of similar objects, for allowances must be made for condition and, indeed, the eagerness of the buyer and the willingness of the seller for the transaction to be made. Nevertheless, valuations given herein have been carefully calculated to give as fair a representation as possible, and may normally be relied upon as providing a reasonable basis for negotiation.

In addition to the brief histories of the factories given herein, individual objects will be found to have been singled out for particular mention in footnotes printed in italics. It is hoped that these will add to the reader's enjoyment and understanding of the fascinating world of porcelain by extending the scope of the book beyond that of a mere catalogue of illustrations and prices realised.

INTRODUCTION

CONTINENTAL PORCELAIN

The Chinese had produced porcelain from around AD 850 and pieces started arriving in Europe from the end of the 12th century. From the late 15th century porcelain was imported into Italy in quite considerable quantities.

ITALIAN PORCELAIN

The Italians were at that time producing maiolica, a tin-glazed earthenware. From the beginning of the 16th century, efforts were made to produce a body similar to the Chinese and in the 1570's a type of artificial or soft-paste porcelain was produced. This Medici porcelain is so rare there are only about 50 pieces extant and so it is hardly something the collector is likely to stumble across!

The first Italian hard-paste porcelain was produced in Venice from 1721-27, by Francesco Vezzi. This porcelain is very rare. Geminiano Cozzi founded another factory in Venice in 1764 and this lasted until 1812. Cozzi tended to copy wares of other factories. There was a factory at Le Nove which produced porcelain from 1765-1825. The wares of Le Nove are very similar to those of Venice. The pastes are virtually indistinguishable.

The factory at Doccia was founded by Carlo Ginori in 1735, although only small quantities of a very experimental porcelain were produced until 1746. The early porcelain had a very greyish opaque glaze. When Lorenzo Ginori took over the factory in 1757 the paste improved considerably.

Capodimonte is one of the few 18th century European factories to produce soft-paste porcelain. It was founded in 1743. In 1759 the factory was transferred to Buen Retiro outside Madrid.

GERMAN PORCELAIN

The first success at producing a European hard paste or true porcelain was in the first decade of the 18th century in Germany. J. F. Böttger had been experimenting with various pastes, and in around 1709-10 finally produced enough

porcelain to make viable the forming of the Royal Saxon Porcelain Manufactory at Meissen. This porcelain tended to be of a milky colour and it was not until about 10 years later when china-stone was added that the true brilliant white body of Meissen porcelain was finally achieved. From the 1720's the porcelain produced at this factory achieved a consistent standard of excellence, particularly in the quality of the enamel painting. J. G. Herold had been working at the Du Paquier Vienna factory and was persuaded by Stölzel to transfer to the Meissen factory. Herold was responsible for the introduction of these fine enamels. Herold's painting, particularly his Turkish harbour scenes and exquisite chinoiseries, could not be rivalled until J. J. Kändler arrived at the factory in the 1730's. Kändler began decorating table-services, but was soon producing marvellous figures. The factory's heyday ran until the Seven Years War from 1756-63. After the occupation of the factory by troops, the quality of the wares produced deteriorated rapidly. In 1864 the factory was moved to Triebischtal, where it still produces copies of eighteenth century models.

A factory was founded by Claudius Innocentius Du Paquier in Vienna in 1717. Stölzel, a kiln-master from Meissen, joined the Vienna factory in 1719. This factory produced some porcelain of exceptional quality which now commands high prices, due to the quality and rarity. Much of Du Paquier's ware was sold undecorated to *Hausmaler* and this added to the diversity of the wares. One of the characteristics of Du Paquier's porcelain of the 1730's is the strapwork and trellis pattern painted in iron red and other colours. Du Paquier sold the factory in 1744 to the Empress, Maria Theresa. This began the 'State Period' of the factory, when the 'Bindenschild' was used as the mark of the factory. It was usually painted under the glaze but can sometimes be found impressed or incised. In some ways the quality of decoration on the porcelain of this period was sacrificed in order to improve the financial stability of the factory. The Empress appointed J. J. Niedermeyer as chief modeller, and he produced many figure types with the assistance of Grassi and Dannhauser.

In 1784 Konrad von Sorgenthal took over the factory and it began to prosper once again, using basically a Sèvres style decoration.

The factory eventually closed in 1866. Many porcelains catalogued as 'Vienna' dated from the mid to the end of the 19th C. and were made at numerous German factories. As the eighteenth century progressed, more and more workmen gained the secret of hard-paste porcelain and were tempted to other factories. Höchst was started in 1750, Berlin 1751, Nymphenburg 1753, Fürstenberg 1753, Frankenthal 1755 and Ludwigsburg in 1758. These are the main factories, but many other minor factories flourished in Thuringia and many 18th C. wares are known under this vague term. The position is further complicated by decorators moving from one factory to another and wares cannot be attributed to one factory solely by style of decoration.

DUTCH PORCELAIN

Porcelain was produced in Holland at Weesp, Oude Loosdrecht, Amstel and The Hague. Weesp produced porcelain from 1762-1771. Johannes de Mol transferred the factory to Oude Loosdrecht where they continued using the Weesp moulds until they were replaced by the popular Louis-Seize styles. In 1784 the factory was transferred to Oude Amstel where it continued until 1820.

FRENCH PORCELAIN

After various false starts, soft-paste porcelain was certainly produced from c. 1694-1766 at Saint-Cloud by the Chicaneau family. There can be some confusion between this factory and early Chelsea and Derby due to the similarity of the paste. In 1725 Cirou opened a factory at Chantilly which again produced a soft paste porcelain, which tended to be decorated in Kakiemon style. In the early days of the factory a white opaque glaze was applied. By the middle of the century a lead-glaze was applied which much improved the quality of the wares. The factory closed c. 1800. The Mennecy factory, which was actually started in Paris, produced one of the most excellent soft paste porcelains. Production was carried out at Mennecy from 1748-1773. In 1773 the factory moved to Bourg-la-Reine. It closed in 1806.

Many attempts were made at Vincennes to produce a porcelain body, but with little success until around 1745. This porcelain was of the soft paste variety and has quite distinct qualities. Soft-paste was particularly suitable for the more flowing 'softer' lines and the mid 18th C. rococo style found its true expression in the Vincennes porcelain. Soft-paste is an excellent medium for colour painting on porcelain.

One of the other main features of Vincennes was the biscuit figure. The fine modelling of these figures would have been obscured by the thick glazes used on soft paste at this time in France.

By 1756, due to lack of space, the porcelain factory was moved to Sèvres. Vincennes and later Sèvres were indeed lucky to enjoy the patronage of the King, and in 1759 the King actually bought the factory to avoid closure.

The secret of hard-paste or 'true' porcelain was discovered c. 1772 although soft paste was manufactured along with hard paste until the early years of the 19th century.

Many factories opened in Paris in the 1770's and it is often difficult to attribute wares to a particular concern. Hence the generic term 'Paris' which is rather like the 'Staffordshire' of France. Due to the revolution there was a great upheaval in the production of porcelain, however this did lead to some quite innovative stylistic developments.

The developments of the European factories in the eighteenth and nineteenth centuries make a fascinating study. In the early stages the factories were desperately trying to emulate the Chinese, however they rapidly developed individual styles and produced some highly original wares.

9

ALCORA-ANSBACH

A pair of Alcora wine glass coolers, painted with grisaille landscape panels within arabesques and lime green bands, the rims gilt, gilt A marks, c. 1785. **£300-400**
A good example of the restrained neo-classical style.

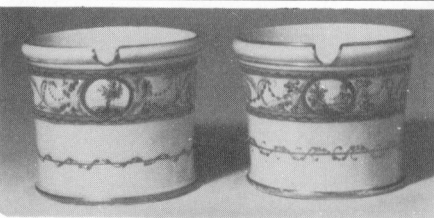

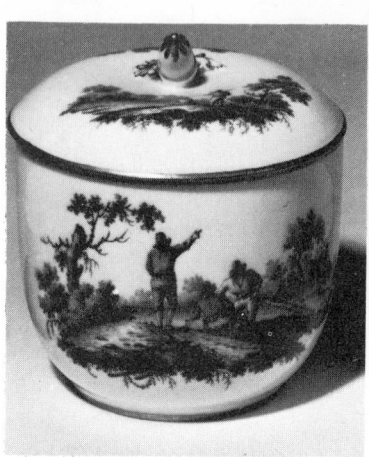

An Amstel circular sugar bowl and cover with acorn finial, painted in brown monochrome with figures in extensive rural landscapes, cover chipped, hair crack, blue script mark, c. 1780, 11 cm. high. **£200-300**
Amstel favoured pastoral or figural vignettes (i.e. lacking defined borders). Note particularly the foliage pendant from the lower edge of the painting.

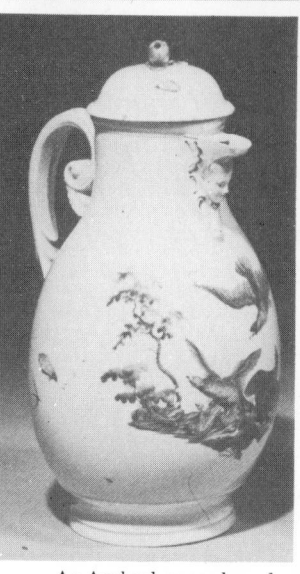

An Ansbach pear-shaped coffee pot and cover, the front painted in colours with a golden eagle descending on a group of game birds and chicks in a landscape, the sides with insects, small chips to cover and spout, 23 cm. high, blue A mark, c. 1765, chain attachment to cover. **£750-£1,000**
The heavy baluster (or pear-shape) coffee pot is a form common to most German factories from about 1740-70.

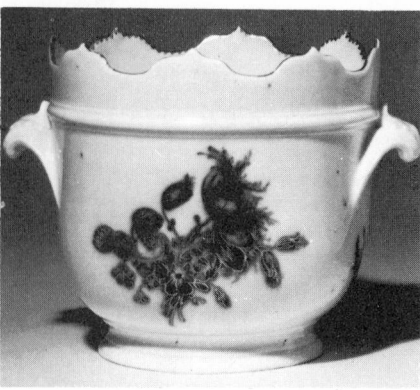

An Ansbach two-handled ice pail, painted with sprays of blue flowers and with scattered insects, edged with gilding and with gilt dentil rim, blue A mark, c. 1770, 17.5 cm. wide **£800-£900**

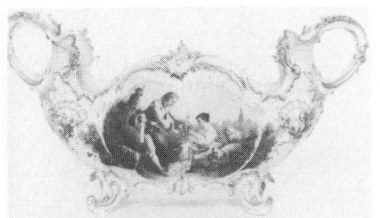

A Berlin centre bowl, the borders moulded and gilt with rococo foliate scrolls forming the feet, rim and handles, 49 cm., sceptre in underglaze-blue, printed orb and KPM, c. 1900. **£300-400**
This piece is typical of the late 19th C. German neo-rococo wares.

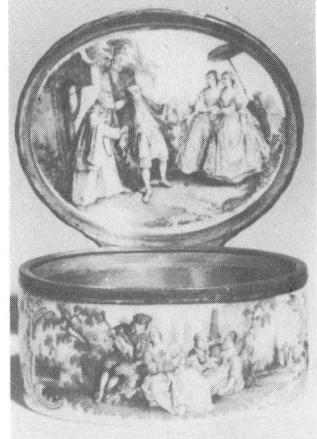

A Berlin snuff box and cover, with gilt metal mounts, painted with Watteau figures within moulded pink foliage scroll cartouches, perhaps c. 1775, 8 cm. wide. **£800-950**

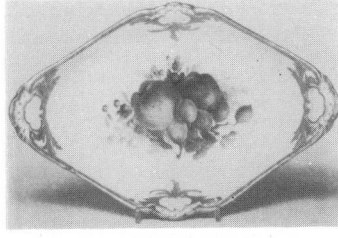

A late 19th C. Berlin fruit bowl, with gilt scroll rim, sceptre in underglaze-blue, printed orb and KPM. **£160-230**

BERLIN

- factory started in 1752 by W. K. Wegely
- produced a hard paste porcelain with poor translucency
- most of styles derived from Meissen and Vincennes
- figures tend to be very heavy with large heads

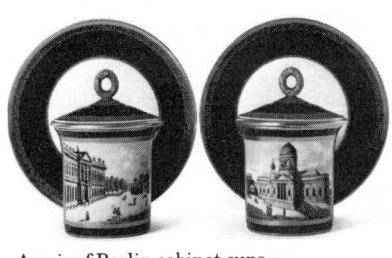

A pair of Berlin cabinet cups, covers and saucers, painted with a panel of 'Strasse Unter den Linder mit Zeughaus' or 'Die Domkirche zu Berlin' on a green ground, the borders and foliate handle gilt, saucer: 17.4 cm., sceptre in underglaze-blue, painted titles, c. 1870. **£650-850**

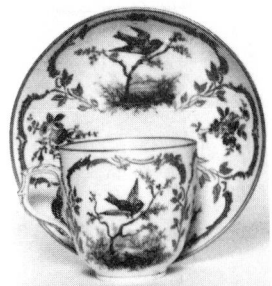

A Berlin cup and saucer, painted with colourful birds, between gilt leaf and foliate scroll borders, saucer: 12.6 cm., sceptre in underglaze-blue, late 19th C. **£90-120**

11

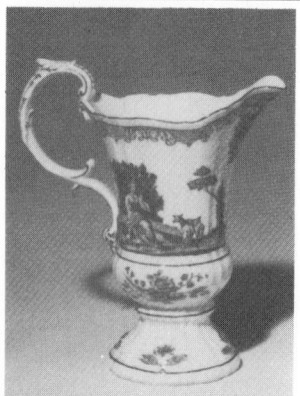

A Berlin armorial Hausmalerei ewer, with scroll handle edged in puce and with a lambrequin border, painted with the crowned arms of Saxony and Poland within gilt foliate cartouche, with iron-red, green and yellow flower sprays between chocolate lines, blue sceptre mark and incised III, c. 1765, 18 cm. high. **£1,000-1,500**
The painting resembles that of F. F. Mayer von Pressnitz, although the quality of the brush strokes suggests that it may only be the work of a follower. Hausmalerei on Berlin is rare.

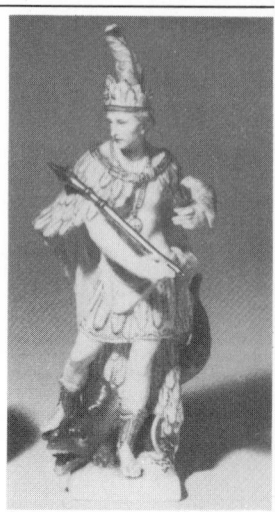

A Berlin figure of America from a set of the Continents, modelled by F. E. Meyer, blue sceptre mark, c. 1770, 28.5 cm. high. **£500-700**

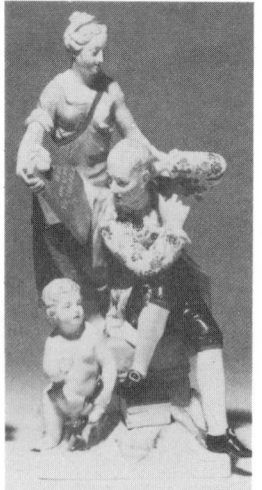

A Berlin group of 'Arithmetic', from the set of the sciences, modelled by W. C. Meyer, minor damage, blue sceptre mark and impressed T, c. 1765, 30.5 cm. high. **£600-700**

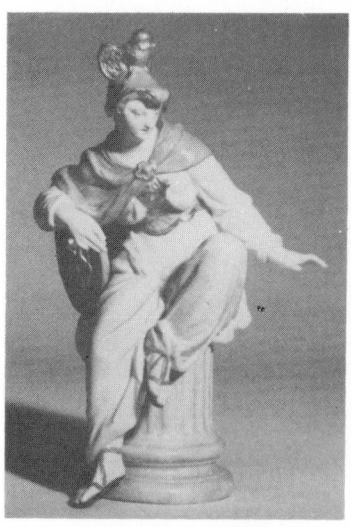

A Berlin figure of Athena, modelled by F. E. and W. C. Meyer, her blue helmet surmounted by a burnished gilt owl, in salmon pink cloak and yellow dress, her blue shield with the face of Medusa, blue sceptre mark, c. 1770, 25 cm. high. **£600-900**

BERLIN

- a second factory was started in 1761 by J. E. Gotzkowsky
- many artists came from Meissen including F. E. Meyer
- porcelain has a distinctly creamy tone
- painting was in the restrained rococo manner
- pieces with Mosaik (or scale pattern) borders and delicate flower painting
- from 1770 the porcelain has a much colder more brilliant white tone
- the factory became influenced by the Neo-classical movement
- figure modelling was perfected by the brothers Friedrich Elias Meyer and Wilhelm Christian Meyer — note the characteristic small heads and elongated bodies
- c. 1775 figure bases became more architectural in design, notably oval and square pedestals
- in the early 19th C. the 'Empire' style of Sèvres was copied
- as the 19th C. progressed Berlin tended to follow the prevailing trends

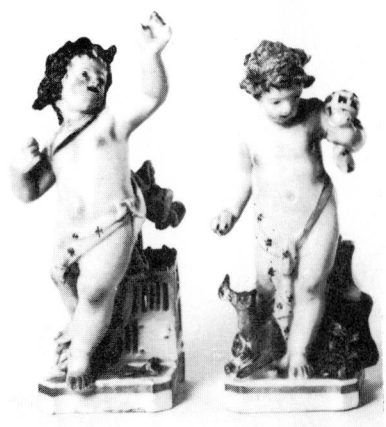

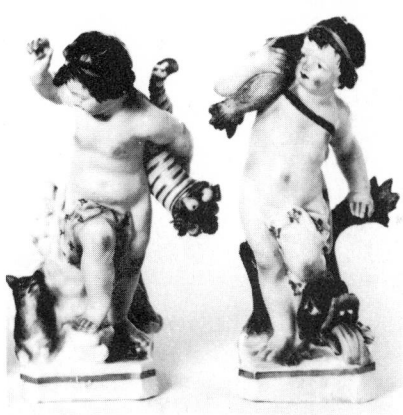

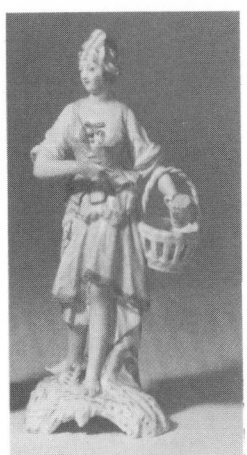

A set of four Berlin figures of the Elements, 'Fire' with a dragon at his feet, 'Water' carrying a fish, 'Air' with a bird-cage and 'Earth' with a fox and a cornucopia of fruits, one repaired, chips, 19 to 20.5 cm., sceptre in underglaze-blue, impressed numerals, mid to late 19th C. **£250-400**

A Berlin figure of a woman, in a puce and yellow striped scarf, white shirt, buff bodice and puce skirt, on scroll moulded mound base edged in ochre, repairs to basket and right hand, blue sceptre mark and Pressnummer 04, c. 1780, 23.5 cm. high. **£400-£500**

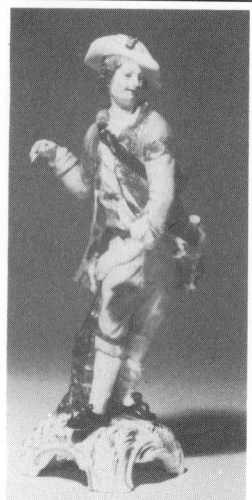

A Berlin figure of a sportsman, modelled by F. E. Meyer, wearing yellow hat, iron-red jacket, green shirt and breeches enriched with gilding, on high gilt foliage-moulded base, c. 1770, 23 cm. high. **£400-550**

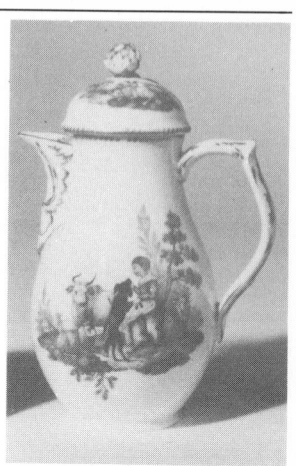

A Berlin baluster hot-milk jug and domed cover, finial restruck, blue sceptre mark, c. 1770-80. **£500-650**

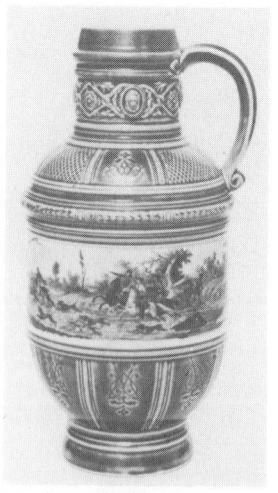

A Berlin porcelain jug, in Raeren style, well painted on a brown ground, 35 cm., sceptre in underglaze-blue, incised marks and numeral, c. 1870. **£300-350**

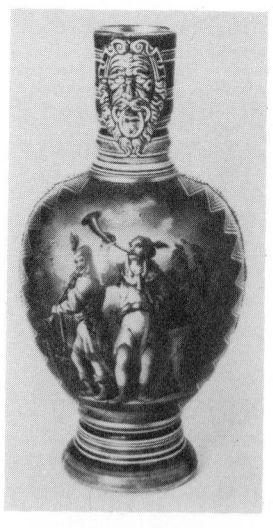

A Berlin jug, painted in sepia with a musical trio, within gilt dentil and moulded borders, underglaze-blue sceptre and printed red orb mark, 50 cm., c. 1880. **£290-350**

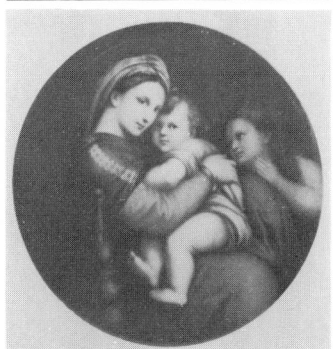

A large circular Berlin plaque, painted after Raphael with the 'Madonna del Sedia', in a muted palette, 35.5 cm. diam., impressed KPM and sceptre, late 19th C., framed. **£400-600**

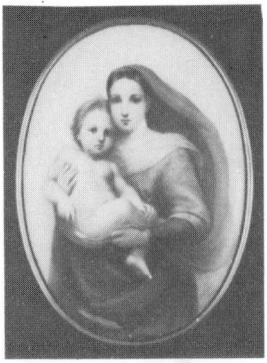

A Berlin plaque, painted by E. Eckardt, signed, after Raphael, with the Madonna and Child in a chiaroscuro of pastel enamels, impressed KPM and sceptre, U.4, late 19th C., 23 cm., velvet-covered mount. **£250-400**

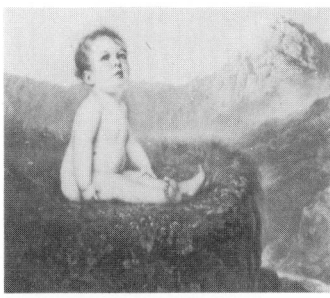

A Berlin plaque, painted by Wagner, signed, impressed sceptre and KPM, impressed numerals, later inscribed 'Sounds from Heaven', 18.5 by 21 cm., late 19th C. **£500-700**

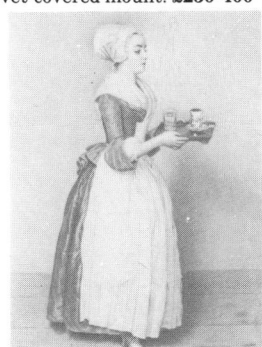

A Berlin plaque painted by Ems, signed, after Liotard, with 'La Belle Chocolatiere', 25.2 by 19.1 cm., impressed KPM and sceptre, late 19th C. **£600-800**

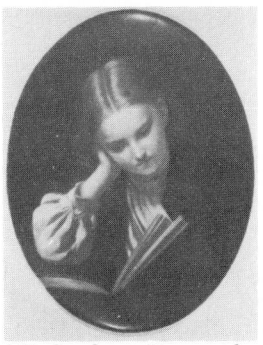

A Berlin plaque, impressed sceptre mark and KPM, mid 19th C., 27.7 cm., framed. **£800-£1,000**

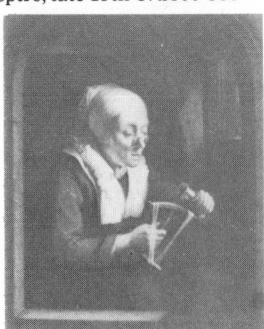

A Berlin plaque, painted after Gerard Doux, impressed KPM and sceptre mark, mid 19th C., 32 by 25.5 cm., framed. **£700-850**

15

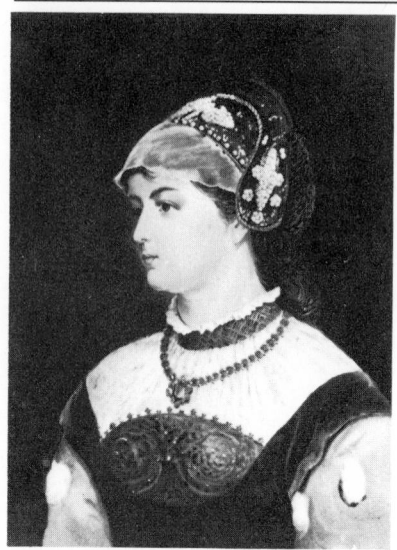

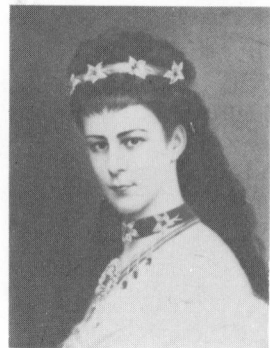

A Berlin rectangular plaque, impressed KPM and sceptre, H, late 19th C., 28 by 22.5 cm., framed. **£450-600**

A Berlin plaque, painted with a young lady, said to be Isabella of Spain, after Holbein, impressed KPM and sceptre, incised numerals, late 19th C., 25 by 19 cm. **£200-300**
This plaque was probably outside decorated.

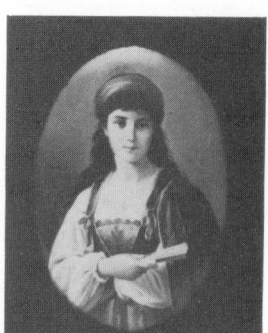

A Berlin oval plaque, impressed sceptre and KPM, 22.7 cm., late 19th C., framed. **£300-500**

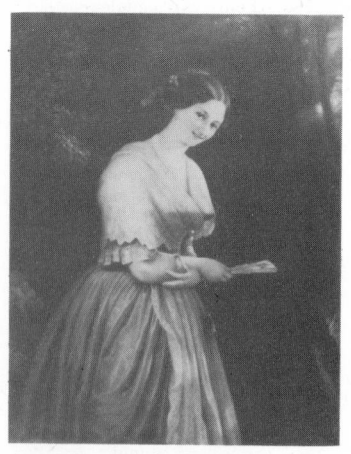

A Berlin plaque, impressed sceptre and KPM, 31.5 by 25.7 cm., late 19th C., framed. **£600-900**

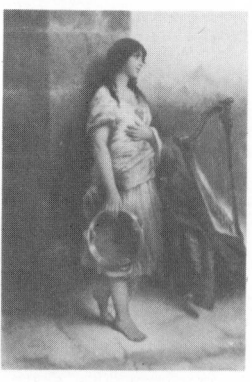

A Berlin plaque, painted by V. Greiner, signed, impressed KPM and sceptre, incised numerals, late 19th C., 23.7 by 16 cm., framed. **£600-900**

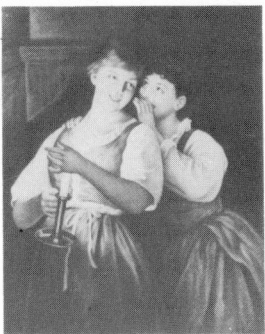

A Berlin plaque, painted by R. Dittrich, signed, with 'A Secret', impressed KPM and sceptre, Sz, incised 315-255, painted title, late 19th C., 31.6 by 26 cm., giltwood frame. **£600-800**

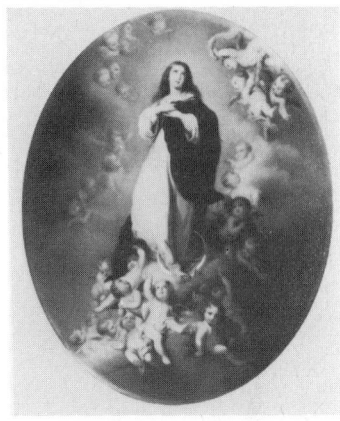

A large Berlin oval plaque, painted by H. Schweizer, signed, with 'The Virgin of the Immaculate Conception', after Murillo, 42.7 cm., impressed KPM and sceptre, late 19th C., framed **£600-1,000**

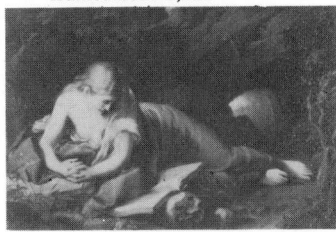

A Berlin plaque, painted with the 'Penitent Magdalene', after Battoni, 15.9 by 24 cm., impressed KPM and sceptre, late 19th C. **£500-700**

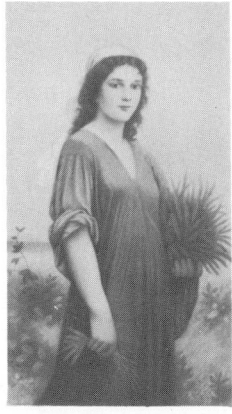

A good and large Berlin plaque, painted by R. Dittrich, signed, with 'Ruth' after Landelle, impressed KPM and sceptre, incised 4.85-2.90, painted title, 48.5 by 29 cm., late 19th C., giltwood frame. **£1,500-2,000**

A good and large Vienna-decorated Berlin plaque, painted by F. Wagner, signed, after Hans Makart, with scene of the Goddess Diana with her handmaidens, 30 by 55 cm., impressed sceptre and KPM, painted shield and title, c. 1880, in a gilt-bronze Empire style frame. **£3,000-5,000**

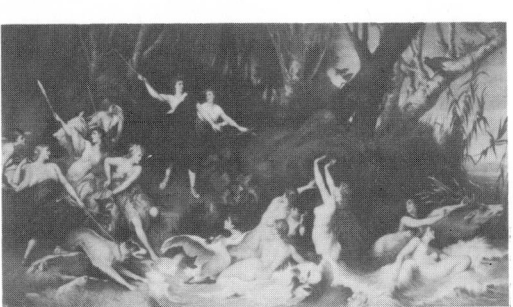

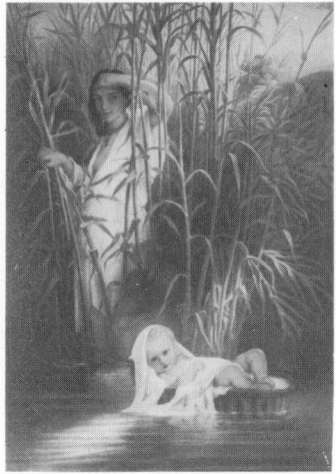

A good and large Berlin plaque, painted after Sturm with 'Moses', 56 by 41 cm., impressed KPM and sceptre, incised numerals, painted title, mid 19th C., framed. **£3,000-4,000**

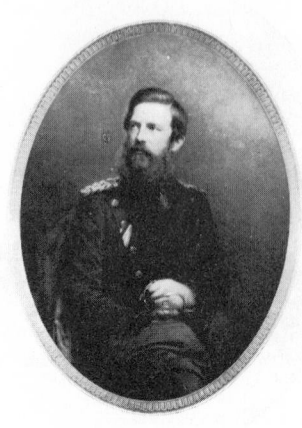

A Berlin plaque, painted in subdued palette with a tooled gilt border, 27.3 cm., impressed KPM and sceptre, 5, c. 1880. **£250-320**

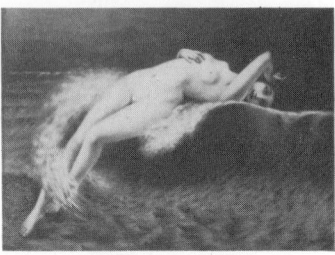

A Berlin plaque, painted by R. Dittrich, signed, with 'The Wave', impressed KPM and sceptre, printed title, 21.5 by 27.5 cm., c. 1900, framed. **£1,000-£1,500**

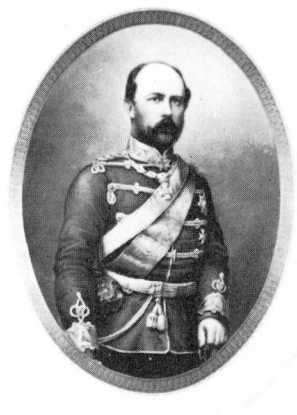

A Berlin plaque, with tooled gilt border, 27.3 cm., impressed KPM and sceptre, F, 5, c. 1880. **£250-£350**

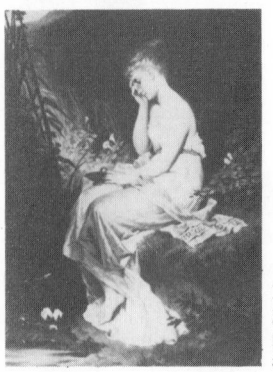

A Dresden-decorated Berlin plaque, impressed KPM and cancelled sceptre, incised 9.6, 23.5 by 16.2 cm., mid 19th C. **£450-650**

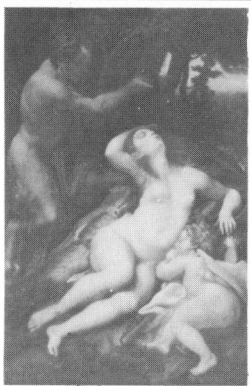

A good Berlin rectangular plaque, painted by E. Bohm, Paris, signed and dated 1863, with 'Le Sommeil d'Antiope', after Corrège, 33.8 by 23.5 cm., impressed KPM and sceptre, 1863, in a giltwood frame. **£2,000-3,000**

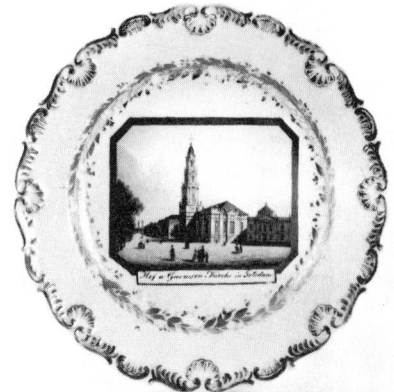

A Berlin topographical plate, painted with 'Hof u: Garnison — Kirche in Potsdam', gilding rubbed, 22.3 cm., eagle, sceptre and KPM in underglaze-blue, c. 1845. **£160-200**
Topographical subjects were popular both at Berlin and Meissen in the mid 19th C.

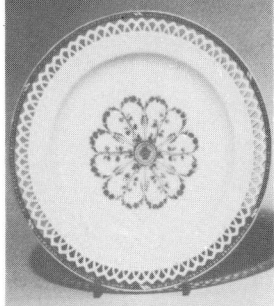

One of 12 Berlin plates, blue sceptre mark to each piece, 24.5 cm. high, c. 1795. **£2,000-2,500** for 12

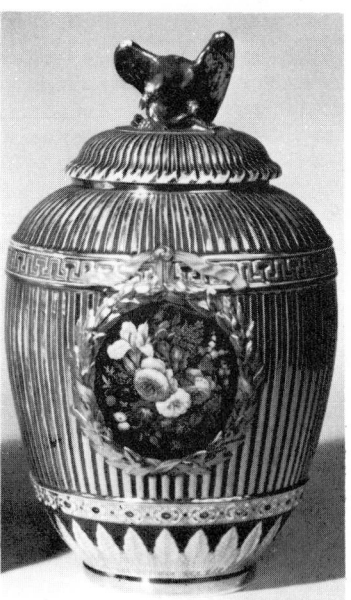

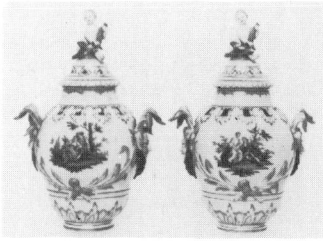

A pair of Berlin pot pourri vases and covers, sceptre in underglaze-blue, 33 cm., late 19th C. **£400-£550**

A pair of late Berlin oviform vases and covers, decorated against a pale blue and gilt fluted grounds, one finial repaired, 37 cm. high. **£600-700**

19

BERLIN-CAPODIMONTE

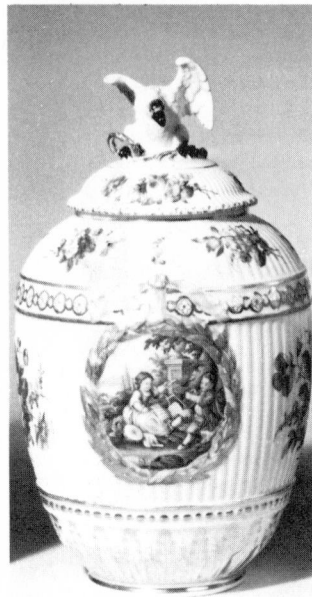

BUEN RETIRO

- **factory founded in 1759, near Madrid**
- **craftsmen were brought from Capodimonte**
- **early pieces are very similar to Capodimonte**
- **produced a soft paste porcelain with a creamy tone**
- **relied heavily on Chinoiserie decoration**
- **ceased to import materials from Italy in the 1770's**
- **porcelain now took on a distinctive yellow tone**
- **in 1784 a fine clear white paste was introduced**
- **factory closed in 1808**

A pair of late Berlin fluted oviform vases and covers, the lower parts gilt with stiff leaves, the domed covers with eagle finials, one finial with slight restoration, 35.5 cm. high. **£300-£450**

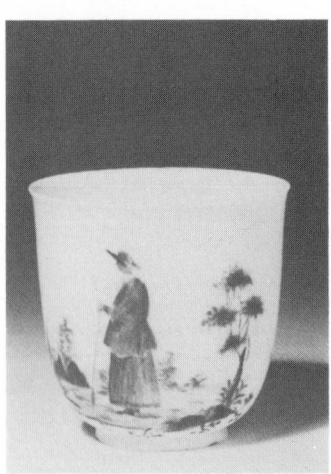

A Capodimonte beaker, painted in soft colours, Fleur-de-lys mark in underglaze-blue, incised n, 6.5 cm. **£520-620**

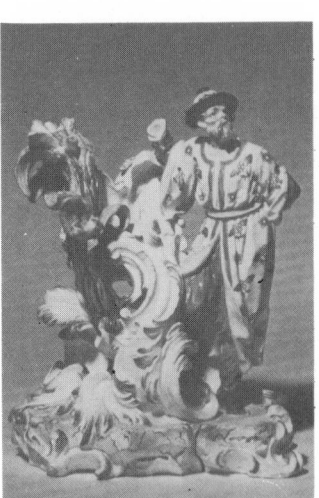

A Buen Retiro Chinoiserie figure, in black hat, flowered coat and lilac breeches, the base with foliage and rococo scrolls enriched in puce, c. 1755, firing crack to base, right hand missing, repair to neck, foliage and base chips, 26.5 cm. high. **£500-700**
The somewhat heavy and rather clumsy modelling are typical.

CAPODIMONTE

- factory founded in 1743

- body clear white soft paste, with good translucency (although sometimes covered in a thick glaze)

- modeller Giuseppe Gricci was responsible for the Commedia dell'Arte figures and some beautiful peasant groups

- figures have small heads
- painting characterised by strong colours and stippled brush strokes

- in 1759 the factory moved to Buen Retiro in Spain

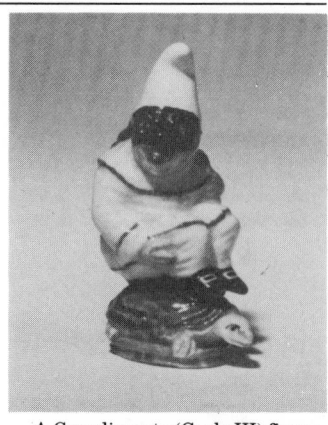

A Capodimonte (Carlo III) figure of a Callot dwarf, in white peaked hat, black mask and blue edged white tunic, seated on a tortoise, c. 1750, 8 cm. high. **£800- 1,000**

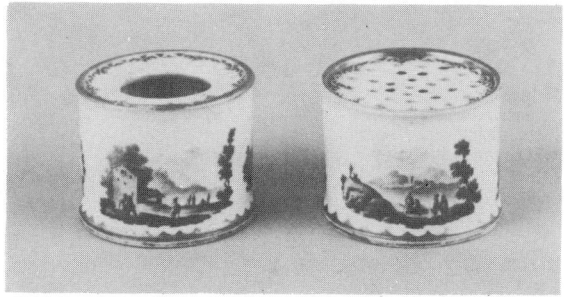

A Capodimonte (Carlo III) inkwell and sander, painted by Guiseppe della Torre, each piece with three vignettes and with gilt scroll borders to the tops, 6.5 cm. diam., traces of blue Fleur-de-lys marks, c. 1750. **£1,000-1,500**

CHANTILLY

- factory founded in 1725 by the Prince de Conde
- up to the 1750's milk white soft paste porcelain produced
- an opaque tin glaze was used until mid 1730's
- beautiful white finish inspired by Japanese porcelain
- Kakiemon style is most typical of early Chantilly wares
- in the mid 18th C. European floral styles introduced, particularly 'deutsche Blumen' — the natural German flowers

- in 1750's a transparent lead glaze was introduced to compete with Vincennes
- wares tended to be rather sparsely decorated in underglaze-blue
- from 1755-80 many floral designs produced, often in one colour, like the 'Chantilly sprig' (like a cornflower), which was then copied by many other factories, e.g. Caughley
- the factory had great problems from the 1780's and had closed by the end of the century

21

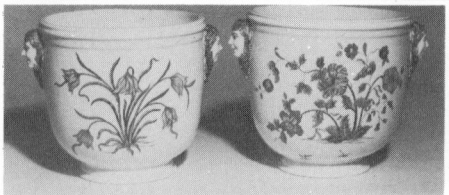

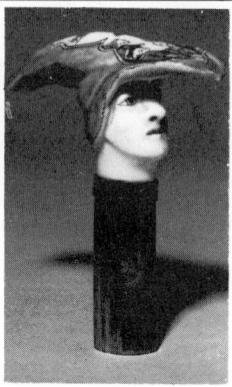

A pair of Chantilly Kakiemon two-handled cache pots, the handles modelled as female masks, painted with brightly coloured flowering plants and scattered insects, one base drilled and restored, iron-red hunting horn marks, c. 1750, 17 cm. high. **£2,000-2,300**
Although the palette is Kakiemon, the naturalistic painting is atypical.

A Chantilly cane handle, modelled as the head of a man in peaked green cap, the top of his hat painted with Chinoiserie figures, hat chipped, c. 1740. **£150- 200**

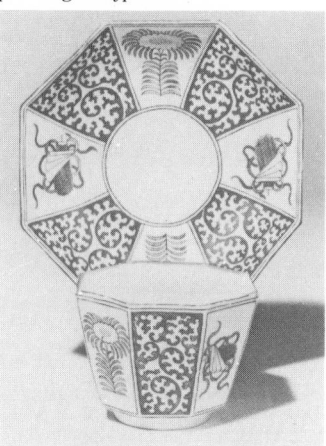

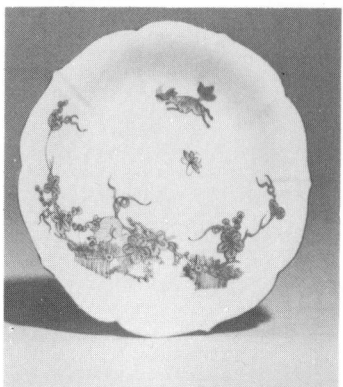

A Chantilly Kakiemon octagonal teabowl and saucer, chocolate mock Chinese seal mark within a circle, c. 1735. **£360-420**

A Chantilly Kakiemon shaped cinquefoil small saucer dish, painted with the 'Flying Fox' pattern within a brown rim, iron-red hunting horn mark, c. 1740, 11.7 cm. diam. **£350-450**

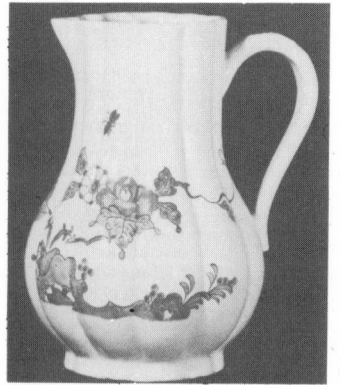

A Chantilly Kakiemon fluted pear shaped jug, painted with flowering peonies issuing from rockwork, c. 1735, 14.5 cm. high. **£700-1,000**
Chantilly, along with St. Cloud, utilised the Kakiemon palette and designs fashionable in the second quarter of the 18th C. Whilst St. Cloud has a creamy lustrous appearance, Chantilly has a flatter look as a result of the application of tin glaze to the surface of the porcelain.

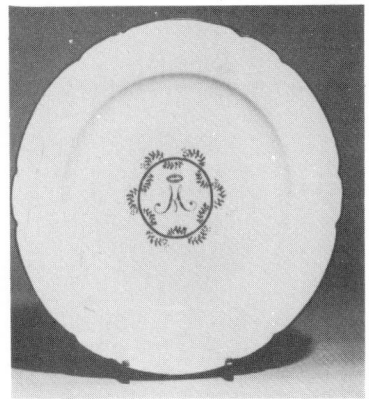

A pair of Chantilly blue and white lobed plates, painted with the initial M within a floral medallion, the rims edged in blue, blue horn and B mark, c. 1765, 24.5 cm. diam. **£150-180**

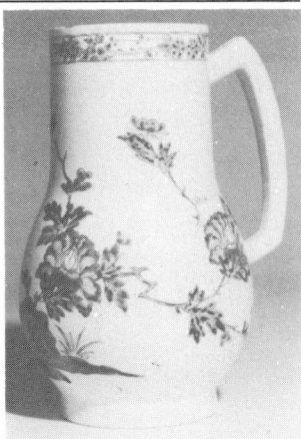

A Chantilly Kakiemon slender baluster jug, painted with flowering prunus issuing from rockwork, in rich blue, green and iron-red colours, chip and 2 cm. crack to interior of rim, iron-red hunting horn mark, c. 1735, 18 cm. high. **£600-800**

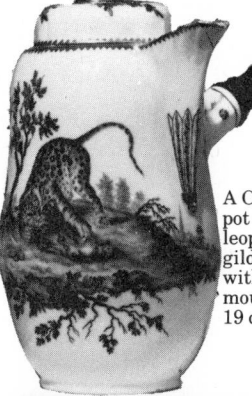

A Copenhagen shaped chocolate pot and cover, painted with leopards and enriched with gilding, blue wave mark, c. 1780, with contemporary gilt metal mounts and ebony handle, 19 cm. high. **£700-850**

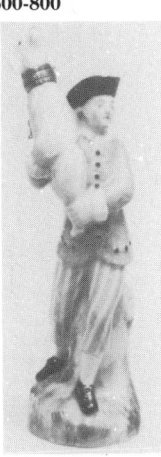

A Copenhagen silver gilt mounted scent bottle and stopper, formed as a youth holding a dog, its head forming the stopper, the silver gilt mounts with chain attachment, blue wave mark at back, c. 1780, 11 cm. high. **£400-£500**

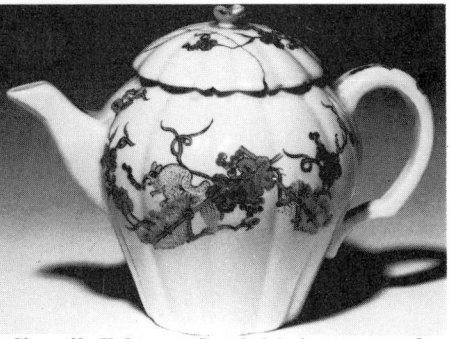

A Chantilly Kakiemon fluted globular teapot and cover, painted with the squirrel pattern, with flower finial, cover repaired, c. 1735, the teapot 15 cm. wide. **£500-600**

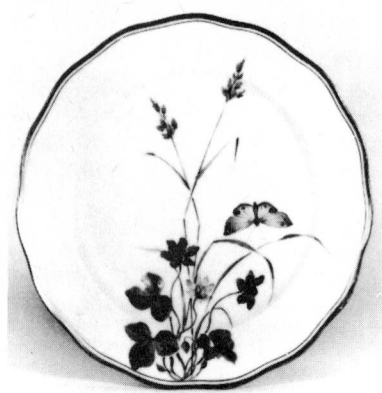

A set of ten Royal Copenhagen plates, in two sizes, the rim moulded with honeycomb pattern within a gilt line border, wave mark in underglaze-blue, c. 1900, 22.4 and 15.6 cm. **£200-£300**

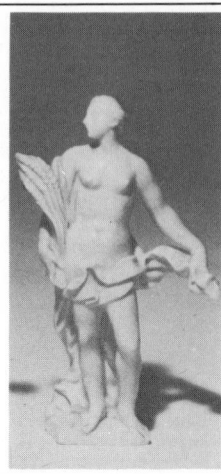

A Doccia Ginori white figure of a nymph, emblematic of Summer, c. 1760, 12.3 cm. high, damaged. **£120-160**

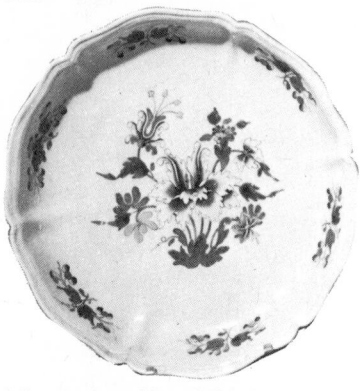

A Doccia shaped hexafoil dish, painted with the 'Tulipano' pattern in bright colours and gilt, 25.5 cm. diam., c. 1760. **£150-250**

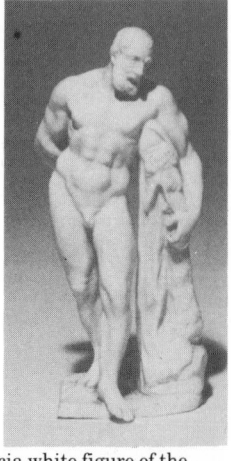

A Doccia white figure of the Farnese Hercules, c. 1760, 14 cm. high, some damage. **£120-£170**

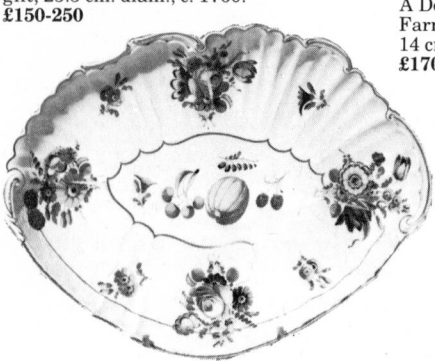

A pair of Doccia shaped oval fluted dishes, half the border with Ozier moulding, the other with flutes, scallops and C-scrolls, painted in bright colours, the rims gilt, c. 1765, 29.5 cm. wide. **£350-450**

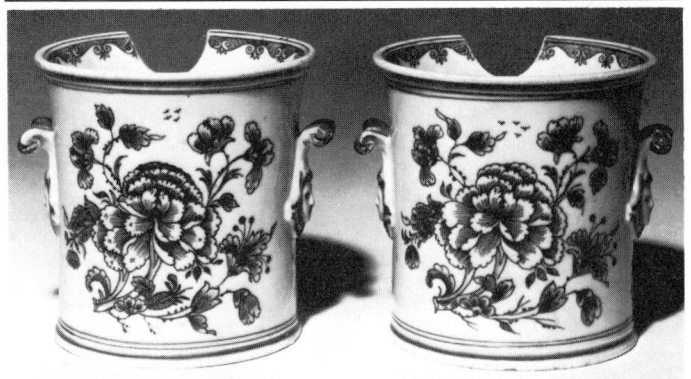

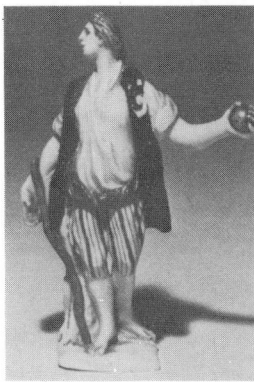

A pair of Doccia blue and white moutardières, the sides painted with chrysanthemum, two handles with slight restoration, one with firing crack to base, c. 1760, 11.5 cm. high. **£250-350**

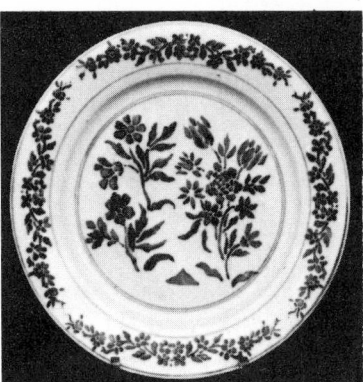

A Doccia figure of Paris holding a golden apple, damage to staff and repair to his jacket, c. 1760, 13 cm. high. **£300-350**
This piece displays the characteristic facial features of Italian porcelain, particularly Doccia and Capodimonte, note the shape of the forehead.

A Doccia 'stampino' blue and white plate, stencilled with sprays of flowers and the border with four garlands, c. 1745, 23 cm. diam. **£500-600**
'Stampino', the application of a paper stencil, is peculiar to this factory.

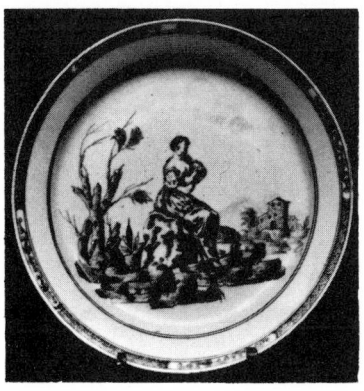

A Doccia blue and white plate, the centre transfer-printed, with cell pattern and foliage border in the Oriental style, star crack to centre, c. 1752, 22.5 cm. diam. **£400-500**

25

DOCCIA

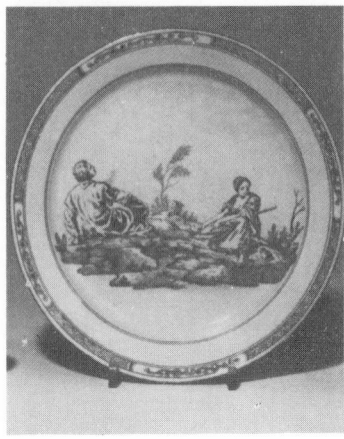

A Doccia blue and white plate, the centre transfer-printed and painted, small crack, c. 1752, 22.5 cm. diam. **£400-500**
Transfer-printing is relatively rare on Continental porcelain.

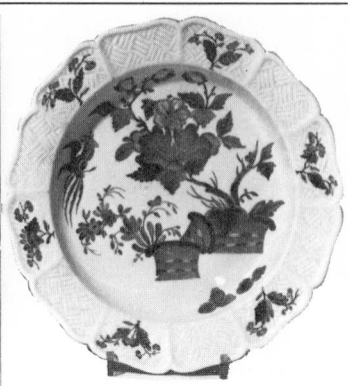

A Doccia shaped circular plate, with Ozier moulded rim, painted in bright enamels with a flying cockerel and scattered flowers, restored, c. 1755, 23 cm. diam. **£350-450**

DOCCIA

- factory started by Carlo Ginori, near Florence in 1735
- hybrid hard-paste porcelain of greyish-white appearance
- body liable to firecracks
- often decorated with mythological, religious and hunting subjects
- glaze can have a 'smudgy' look
- used strong enamel colours
- from 1757-91 the factory was directed by Lorenzo Ginori, glaze and body improved considerably
- figures often in the white and sometimes decorated with an iron-red colour exclusive to the factory
- porcelain often confused with Capodimonte, although Doccia is hard paste and Capodimonte soft paste
- around 1770 figures covered in a white tin-glaze, often firecracked
- in the 19th C. the factory tended to copy its 18th C. styles
- factory still exists

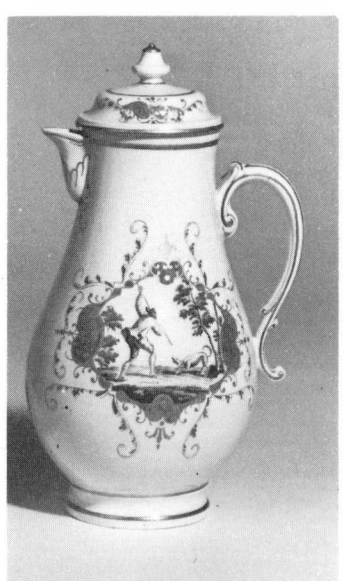

A Doccia 'Alla Sassonia' pear-shaped coffee pot and cover, the gilt C-scroll borders enclosing purple lustre and with iron-red scrolling foliage, c. 1755, 19.5 cm. high. **£500-700**
This piece was possibly from the workshop of Pietro Fanciullacci.

26

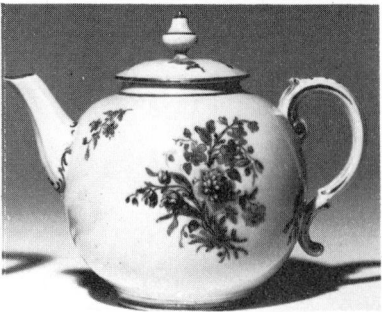

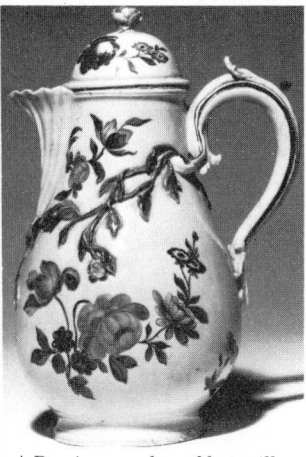

A Doccia pear-shaped hot milk jug and cover, finely painted with bouquets of garden flowers, slight restoration to finial, 1765-70, 20 cm. high. **£1,200-£1,400**

A Doccia polychrome globular teapot and cover, painted with bouquets and scattered garden flowers, the handle, spout and rims enriched with gilding, finial repaired, 1765-70, 17.5 cm. wide. **£450-550**

DRESDEN

The general term Dresden covers many 19th C. factories emulating Meissen. There is a tendency for the 19th C. Dresden factories to employ over-elaborate decoration although the form or model may be similar to its 18th C. prototype.

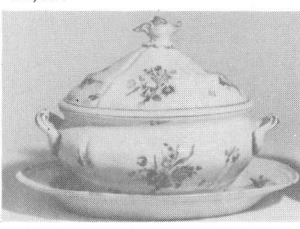

A pair of Doccia two-handled vegetable tureens, covers and stands, painted with bouquets of flowers in colours within puce rims, minor chips to one finial and the underside of one cover, one stand chipped, c. 1760, the stands 30.5 cm. wide. **£700-900**

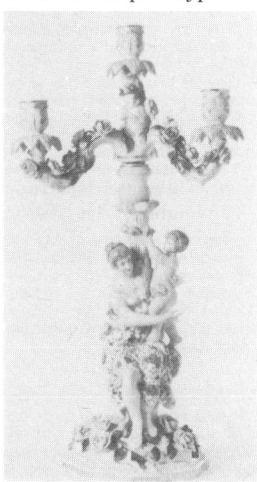

A Dresden four-light candelabrum, minor chips, cross and initials mark in underglaze-blue, 50 cm., c. 1900. **£150-210** *Probably Eckert's factory.*

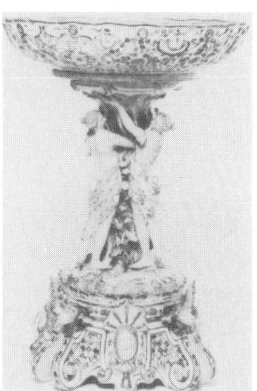

A Dresden centrepiece, with pierced bowl, brightly coloured and with gilt details, painted crossed swords and AR monogram, 40 cm., late 19th C. **£300-350**

DRESDEN

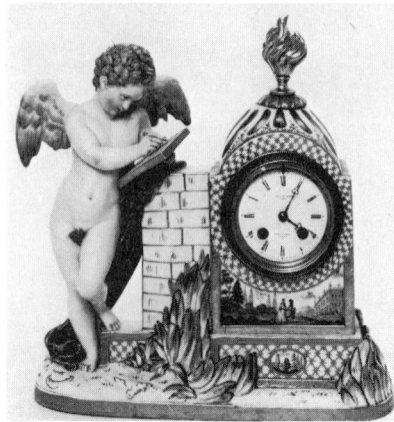

A Dresden clock case, the enamelled dial and movement set in a pedestal, the dial and movement signed Bell and Son, Paris, 27.5 cm., late 19th C. **£250-300**

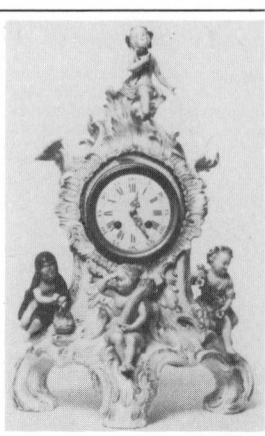

A Dresden clock case, applied with four putti emblematic of 'The Seasons', chips, shield in underglaze-blue, 46 cm., late 19th C. **£400-460**

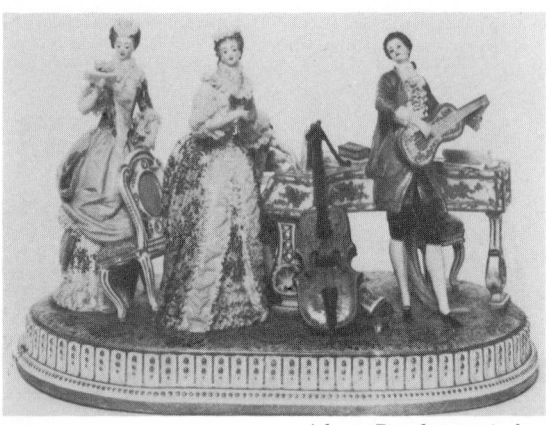

A large Dresden musical group, all in fanciful eighteenth century dress with colourful and lacy details, some damage, crowned mark in underglaze-blue, 40.5 cm. c. 1900. **£300-400**

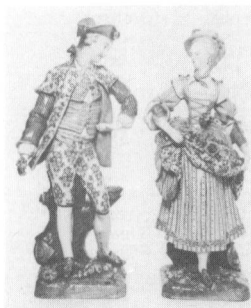

A pair of Dresden figures of a gallant and a lady, chips, crossed swords in underglaze-blue, one incised 'Petit', 50.5 and 49 cm., late 19th C. **£700-800**

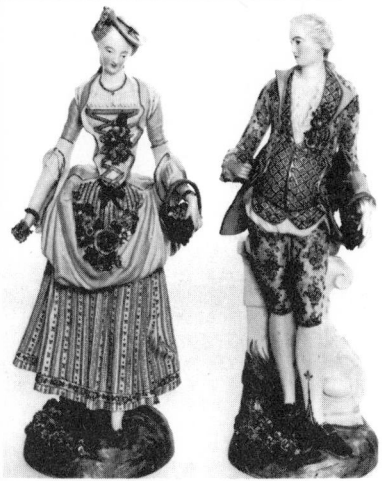

A pair of Dresden figures of a gallant and maiden, in Meissen taste, minor chips, crossed swords in underglaze-blue, 35 and 36 cm., late 19th C. **£300-£350**

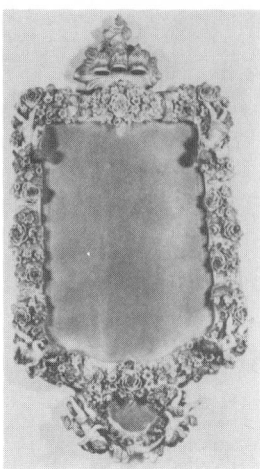

A Dresden mirror frame, fitted at the base with three scrolled branches terminating in foliate sconces, the whole in pastel colours and gilding, two branches damaged, chips, fitted with a bevelled mirror glass plate, 28 cm. overall, late 19th C. **£350-450**

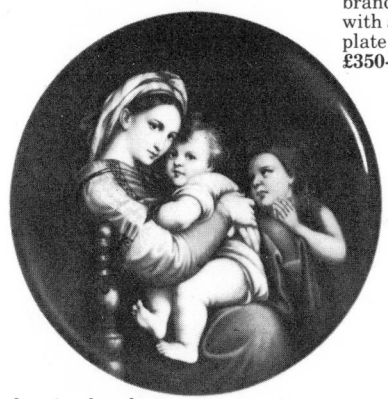

A Dresden circular plaque, painted after Raphael with the 'Madonna del Sedia', in a colourful palette, 17.5 cm., late 19th C., giltwood frame. **£300-£400**

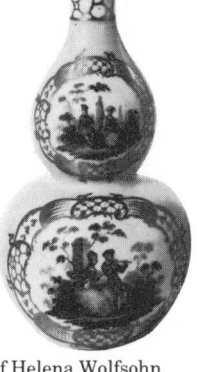

A pair of Helena Wolfsohn yellow ground vases, painted with panels of eighteenth century lovers in gardens within gilt borders, 16.5 cm., AR monogram in underglaze-blue, late 19th C. **£150-200**

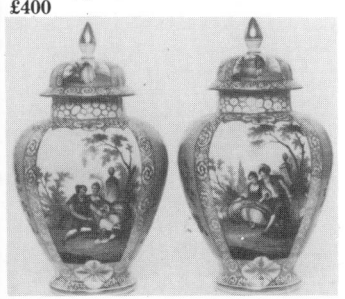

A pair of Dresden vases and covers, on pink grounds between gilt scroll borders, the domed covers with a gilt finial, Dresden and star mark in underglaze-blue, 36.5 cm., late 19th C. **£250-£350**

FRANKENTHAL

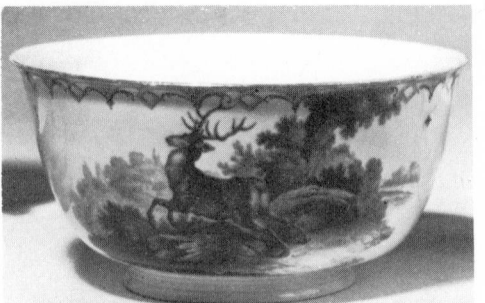

A Frankenthal circular slop bowl, from a Jagd service, painted in brown monochrome, with a yellow and iron-red pendant scroll rim, blue crowned interlaced CT monogram, and dated 1774, 18.5 cm. diam. **£800-1,000**

FRANKENTHAL

- Paul A. Hannong started producing porcelain in Frankenthal in 1755, under the patronage of the Elector Carl Theodor
- glaze has a quite distinctive quality as it tends to 'soak in' the enamel colours
- high quality porcelain produced under Modellmeister J. W. Lanz, who favoured striped gilt grounds and green and crimson
- K. G. Lück and his brother or cousin J. F. Lück came to Frankenthal from Meissen in 1758
- K. G. Lück's work tends to be quite fussy and often on grassy mounds, with rococo edges picked out in gilding
- in the late 18th C. a fine range of figures produced by J. P. Melchior and A. Bauer
- Melchior's figures tend to have a rather severe look
- Frankenthal utility ware is noted for the quality of the painting
- factory closed in 1799
- moulds from the factory were used in many other 19th C. German factories

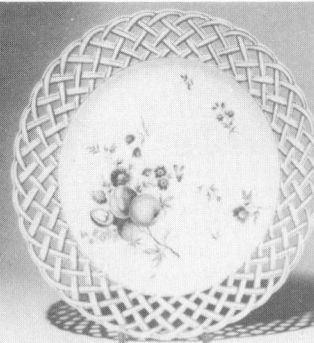

A Frankenthal dish, with pierced border, repaired, blue crowned CT mark and 86, 30 cm. diam., c. 1770. **£700-800**

A Frankenthal figure of a gardener, in white jacket and green breeches, his top-knot restored, the figure and base restuck, blue crowned interlaced CT mark and n. 77, 13.5 cm. high. **£400-500**

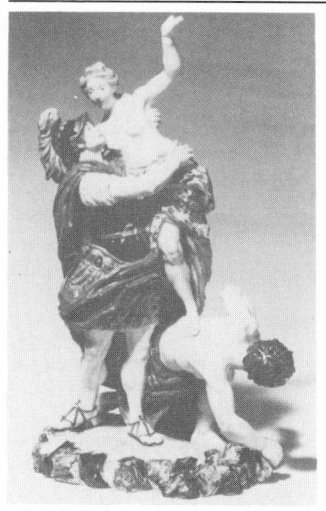

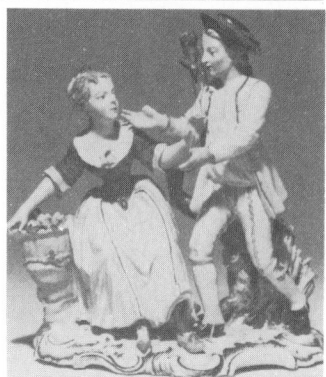

A Frankenthal pastoral group, modelled by J. W. Lanz, some damage and repair work, blue lion rampant mark, 1756-59, 22 cm. high. **£1,500-1,800**

A Frankenthal mythological group of 'The Rape of Proserpine', modelled by J. F. Lück, Pluto in plumed helmet, iron-red cloak and short tunic, with a partially clad man at their feet, on rockwork base, chips to fingers and one hand lacking on kneeling figure, c. 1756, 28 cm. high. **£1,000-1,500**

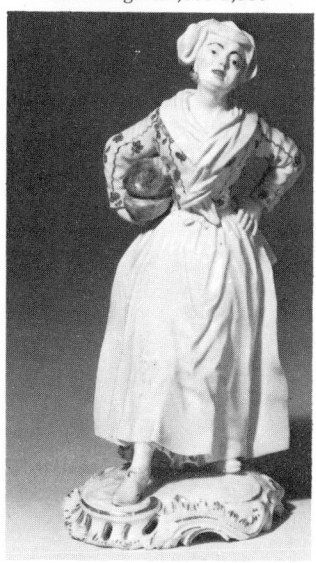

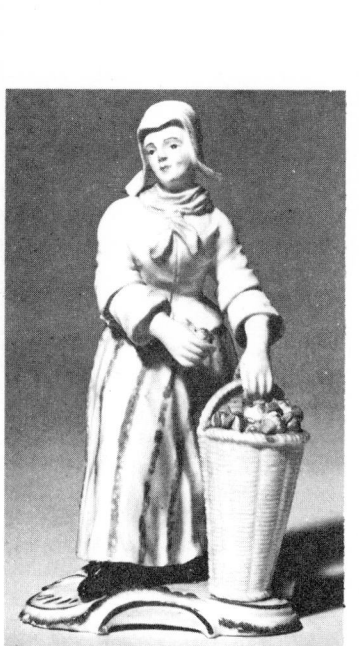

A Frankenthal figure of a baker's wife, on pierced scroll moulded base edged with gilding, minor chips, blue rampant lion mark and monogram mark of Joseph Adam Hannong, 1759-62, 20 cm. high. **£600-800**

Left
A Frankenthal figure of a fruit seller, in white, green, black and puce, blue lion mark and interlaced initials of Joseph Adam Hannong, 1759-62, repair to right hand, 14 cm. high. **£600-700**

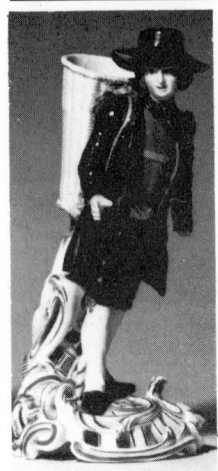

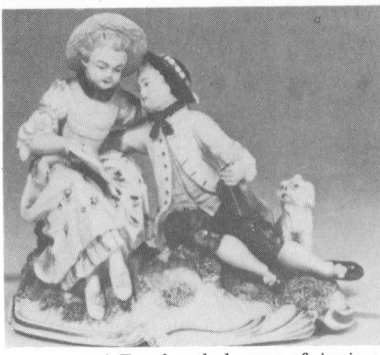

A Frankenthal group of singing children, modelled by Adam Bauer, painted in pastel colours, some damage, blue crowned interlaced CT mark over 71, c. 1771. **£1,100-1,400**

A Frankenthal figure of a journey man, modelled by Joh. Friedrich Lück, in black hat, jacket and breeches and red waistcoat, his hat with repaired chip, the basket restuck, lacks left hand and part of staff, blue crowned CT mark and an incised R, c. 1760, 22 cm. high. **£800-£1,000**

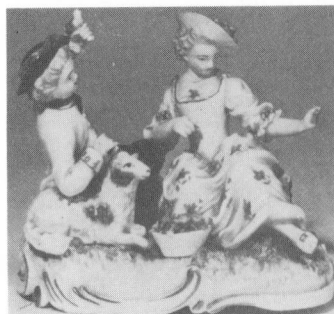

A Frankenthal group of children, modelled by Adam Bauer, some damage, blue crowned interlaced CT mark over 72, c. 1772, 15.5 cm. wide **£800-1,200**

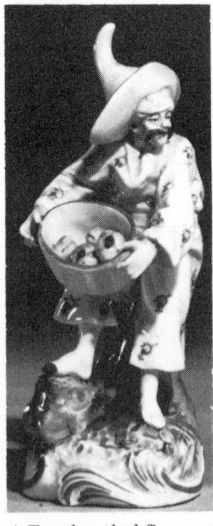

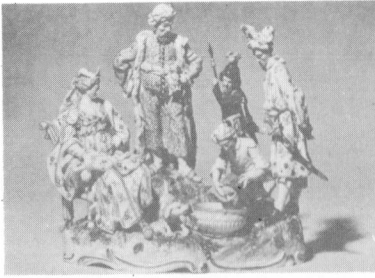

A rare Frankenthal mythological group of Queen Tomyris and the head of Cyrus, probably modelled by Simon Feilner, on a shaped oval foliage-encrusted and scroll-moulded base, enriched in colours and gilding, c. 1773, repairs, 23 cm. wide. **£4,000-6,000**

A Frankenthal figure of a Chinaman modelled by K. G. Lück, on gilt scroll base, blue crown and interlaced CT mark, c. 1770, 12.5 cm. high. **£900-£1,000**

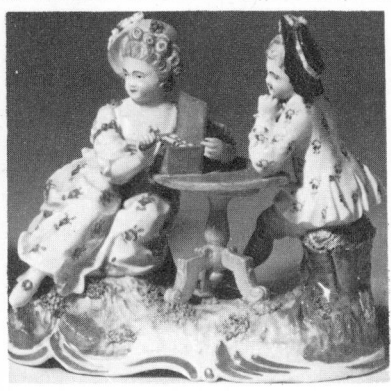

A Frankenthal group of a young boy and girl, modelled by Adam Bauer, edge of table repainted and her right foot restored, blue crowned CT mark, c. 1775, 15.5 cm. wide. **£1,400-1,600** *One of the characteristics of Bauer's work is plump-cheeked children.*

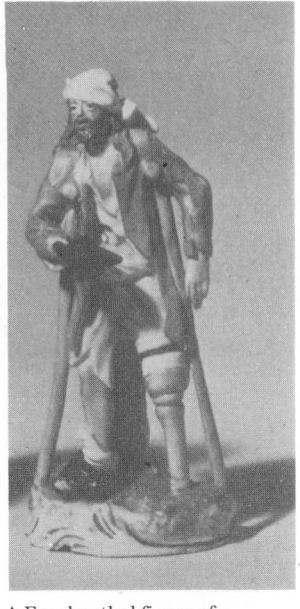

A Frankenthal figure of a beggarman, modelled by K. G. Lück, in green and yellow, repair to his hat, one crutch and the base, blue crowned CT mark and the date 1776, 15.5 cm. high. **£800-1,000**

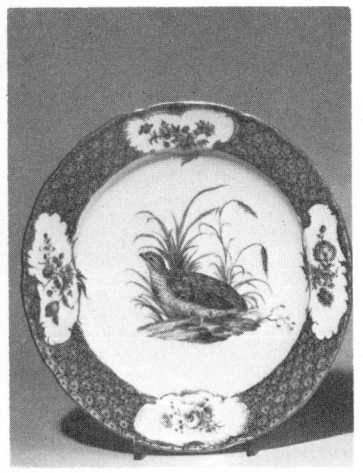

A Frankenthal ornithological plate, painted with a grouse in a landscape vignette, within a puce scaled border reserved with four gilt scrolled panels enclosing flower sprays, blue rampant lion mark, c. 1756-59, 24 cm. diam. **£600-700**

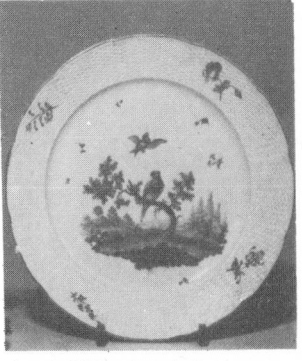

A pair of Frankenthal ornithological plates, with lobed Ozier borders and painted in colours, with gilt rims, blue crowned CT marks, AB monograms, c. 1775, 23 cm. diam. **£800-1,000**

FÜRSTENBERG

FÜRSTENBERG

- factory founded in 1747 but it was not until Johann Benckgraff arrived from Höchst in 1753 that porcelain was produced here
- principal modeller at this period was Simon Feilner
- enamelling technique was not perfected at this factory until the early 1760's, and underglaze-blue remained of poor quality until the late 1760's
- the body remained of a yellow tinge until the 1770's and the glaze tended to speck
- it was these imperfections which encouraged the use of high-relief rococo scrollwork
- other modellers of note are A. C. Luplau, J. C. Rombrich and Desoches
- the factory passed into private ownership in 1859 and still exists today

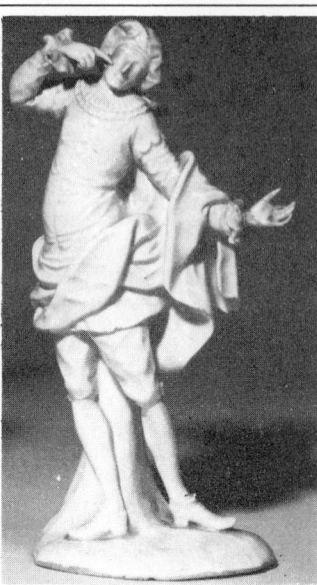

A Fürstenberg white figure of Mezzetin, modelled by Simon Feilner, wrist repaired, incised Ff/O, 1753-54, 19.5 cm. high. **£1,200-1,450**

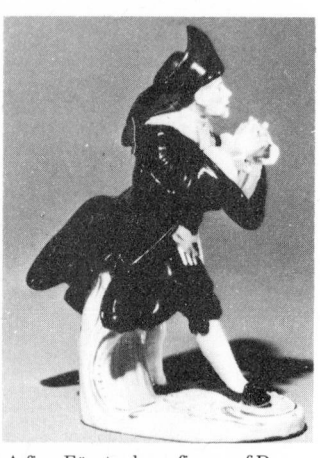

A fine Fürstenberg figure of Dr. Boloardo from the Italian comedy, modelled by Simon Feilner, chips to hat and one finger, blue script F mark and incised C/no 270/J, c. 1760, 12.5 cm. high. **£5,000-7,000**
This figure would appear to be halfway between the Feilner figure illustrated by Ducret: 'Das Fürstenberger Porzellan', vol. 3, fig. 15, and the Luplau model loc. cit., fig. 37.

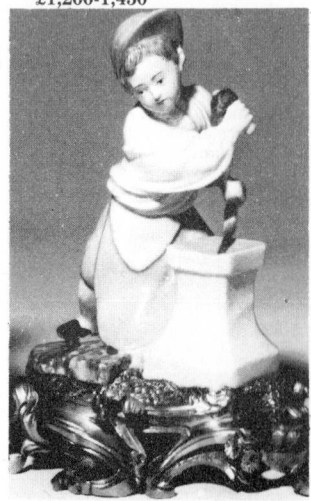

A Fürstenberg figure of Cupid in disguise as Abbé, modelled by S. Feilner, on a shaped gilt scroll-moulded base, lacks wings, chips to fingers, iron-red D, No. 39, c. 1755, 14 cm. high. **£200-£300**
Cf. S. Ducret, 'Unknown Porcelain of the 18th Century', pl. 8.

Right
A Fürstenberg pear-shaped chocolate pot and domed cover with bud finial, painted by Andreas Oettner, in colours and gilt, the scroll moulded spout and moulded handle enriched in gilding, with gilt scroll and foliage border, blue script F mark below the handle, c. 1767, cover damaged, crack and small chip to spout, 11 cm. high. **£650-750**

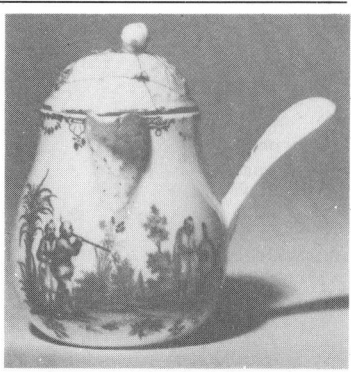

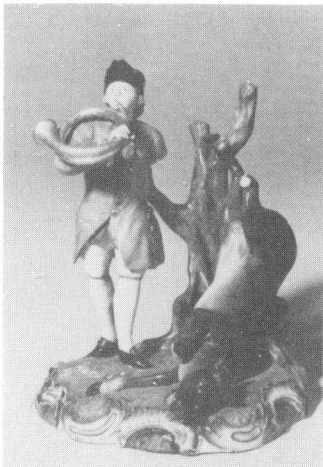

A Höchst group of a huntsman, on a grassy mound base edged with puce and gilt scrolls, damages and repairs, dog missing, blue crowned wheel mark, c. 1765. **£400-500**

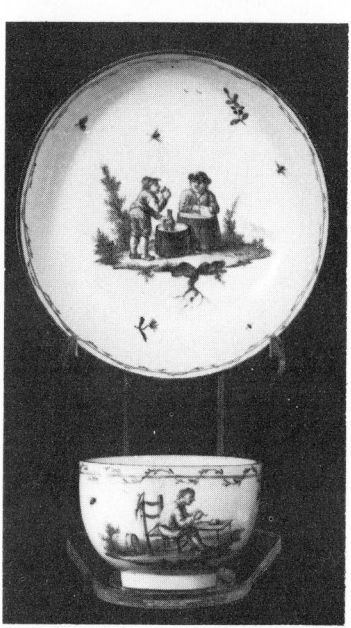

A pair of Höchst teacups and saucers, three of the pieces with two figures, blue wheel mark and various impressed marks, c. 1770. **£1,000-1,200**

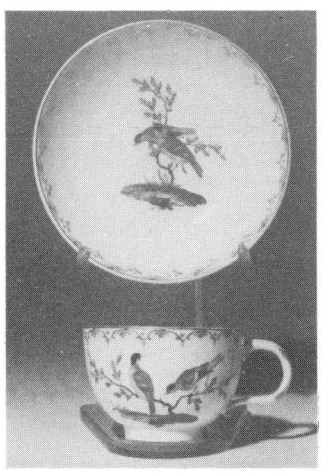

A 'The Hague' teacup and saucer, painted in colours with birds perched on branches within gilt C-scroll borders, blue stork marks, c. 1770. **£350-400**

HÖCHST

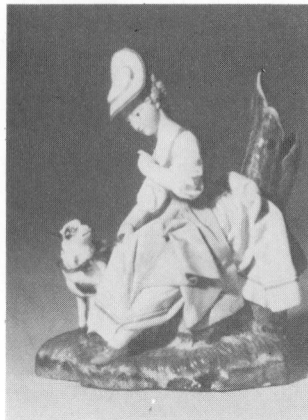

A Höchst figure of a young woman, modelled by J. P. Melchior, seated in a yellow and green hat, green bodice, white shirt, yellow skirt and puce apron, the top of hat restored, blue crowned wheel mark and impressed MA monogram twice, c. 1765. **£800-1,100**

HÖCHST

- factory was founded in 1746 by the painter A. F. von Löwenfinck
- porcelain was produced from 1750
- milk-white in colour
- early wares tended to have poor translucency and be somewhat heavy
- later produced some excellent quality figures under the designer A. F. Riedel
- note the delicately painted sprig patterns
- from 1758-65 the style reminiscent of the French 'Louis Seize' style came into fashion
- this style was continued and developed by J. P. Melchior who was chief modeller 1767-79
- the base of figures from 1765 tends to be in the form of a grassy mound
- the factory closed in 1796

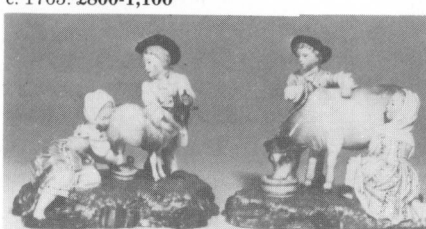

A pair of Höchst milking groups, modelled by J. P. Melchior, some damage on both, one with blue wheel mark, the other with former's marks N50iR, c. 1765, 18.5 cm. wide. **£3,400-3,800**

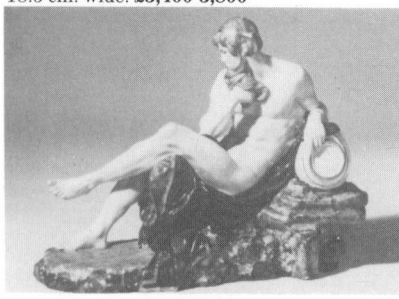

A Höchst figure of a river god, modelled by J. P. Melchior, on a rock and grass mound base, c. 1770, 26 cm. wide. **£1,000-£1,200**

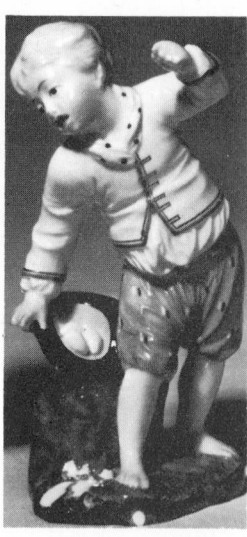

A Höchst figure of a young boy, modelled by J. P. Melchior, in white jacket and puce breeches, on grassy mound base, chips to right hand and edge of hat, blue wheel mark, c. 1770, 12 cm. high. **£300-400**
The Höchst figures of this period are readily identifiable from the palette (if decorated), which utilises soft pastel enamels.

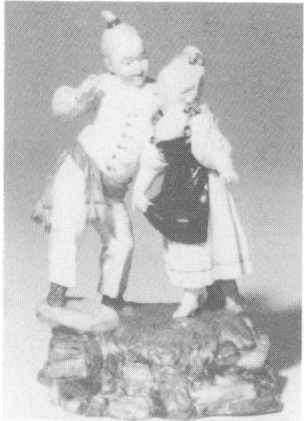

A Höchst group of a Chinese boy and girl, modelled by J. P. Melchior, in white ruff and suit with gilt buttons and gilt fringed pink sash, on high rockwork base, his top-knot chipped and restored, blue crowned wheel mark, c. 1700, 17.5 cm. high. **£1,900-2,200. Perfect: £2,700-£3,000**
The mid 18th C. fascination for Chinoiserie subjects is borne out by the frequent appearance of such subjects in Fürstenberg, Meissen, Höchst and Frankenthal porcelain.

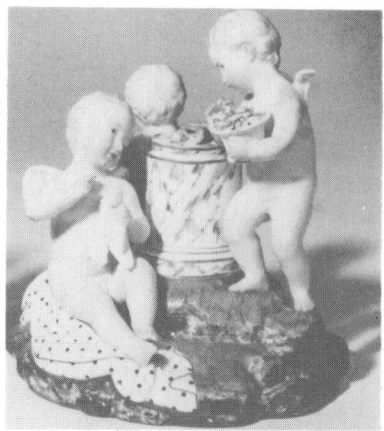

A Höchst group of three Cupids, part of one wing missing, other minor damages, blue wheel mark, c. 1775, 18 cm. wide. **£700-£900**

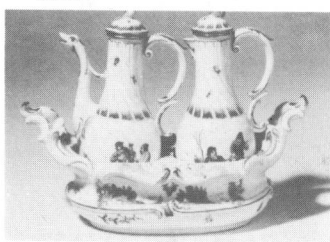

A Höchst porte-huilier, fitted with two baluster ewers and hinged covers with fruit finials, decorated with spiral puce edged moulding to the covers and necks, each piece painted with Teniers scenes, one finial restored, the other restruck, blue crowned wheel marks, the stand with moulded wheel mark and I.H. incised, c. 1765, the stand 24 cm. wide. **£1,500-2,000**

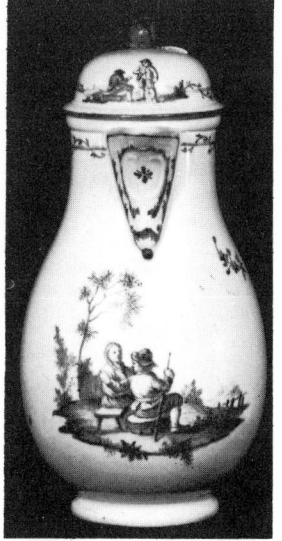

A Höchst milk jug and cover, blue crown wheel mark and incised IN, 18 cm. high. **£1,300-£1,500**

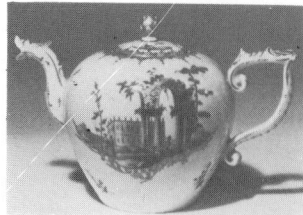

A Höchst teapot, iron-red wheel mark, c. 1755, 18 cm. wide. **£1,400-1,600**
The so-called bullet-shaped teapot is common to all German factories of the mid 18th C.

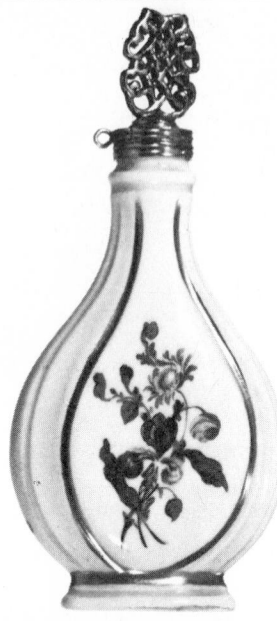

A Höchst scent bottle, with gilt
metal mounts, with monogram
stopper, c. 1760, 9 cm. high.
£250-350

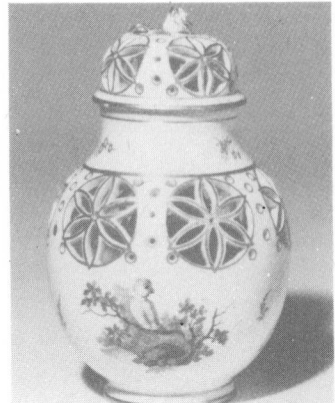

A Höchst pot pourri vase and
domed cover with bud finial,
enriched in gilding and painted
with parrots and cockatoos, the
cover with repair, blue wheel
mark and incised Former's
marks, c. 1765, 18.5 cm. high.
£900-1,100

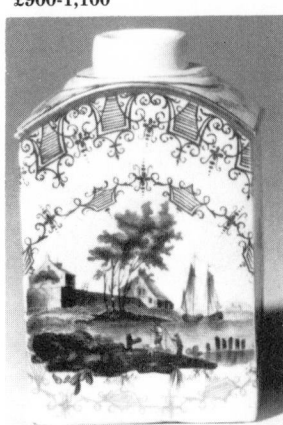

A Höchst arched rectangular
teacaddy, blue wheel mark,
impressed 14 NI, c. 1765, 11 cm.
high. **£550-650**

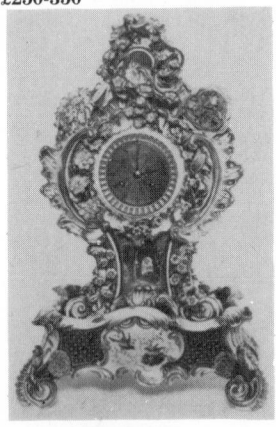

A Jacob Petit clockcase and stand, the
details gilt, chips, 42.5 cm., J.P. in
underglaze-blue, c. 1840. **£300-350**

A pair of Jacob Petit vases, with naturalistically
coloured summer flowers reserved on an apple-
green ground within ornate gilt scroll, foliate
and floral borders, 42 cm., J.P. in underglaze-
blue, c. 1840. **£450-650**
*The extensive use of thickly applied gilding on
claret or apple-green grounds is very typical of
mid 19th C. Paris porcelain.*

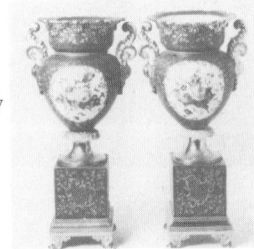

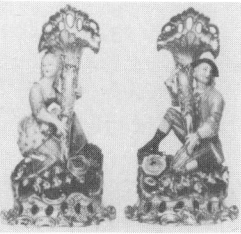

A pair of good Jacob Petit vases, the whole well coloured and gilt, 26.5 cm., J.P. in underglaze-blue, c. 1840. **£280-350**

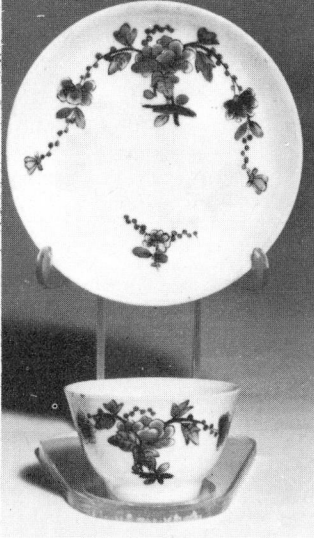

Three Le Nove teabowls and saucers, painted with symmetrical arrangements of famille rose flowers in the Oriental style, various incised marks, c. 1770. **£550-650**

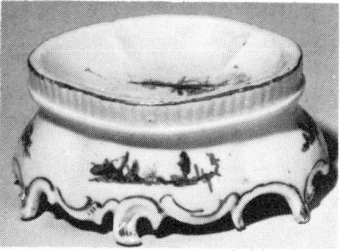

Two Loosdrecht shaped oval quatrefoil trencher salts, painted en camaieu rose with landscape vignettes, birds and flowers, on rococo scroll feet, c. 1700, 9.5 cm. wide. **£200-250**

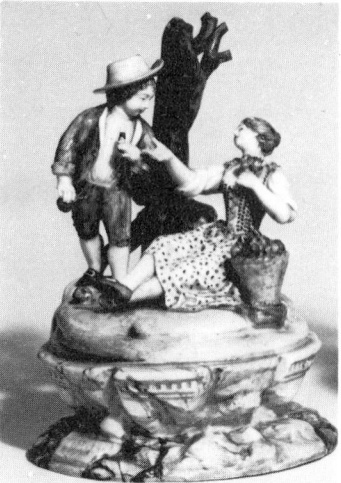

A Le Nove group of two boys and a girl, on high rockwork base with architectural elements, her neck repaired, c. 1780, 18 cm. high. **£700-900**

LE NOVE

- factory established in 1728 near Bassano
- initially made maiolica
- started making a hybrid porcelain in the late 1750's
- wares often painted with masquerade figures
- factory still in existence and probably the most important in Italy today

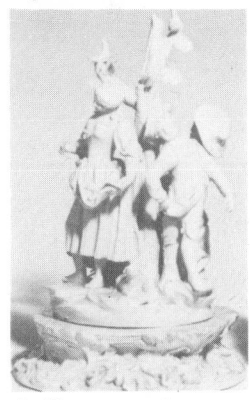

A white Le Nove pastoral group, on detached stand and all on a scrollwork base, one boy with restored feet, c. 1770, 22 cm. high. **£450-650**

39

LOOSDRECHT-LUDWIGSBURG

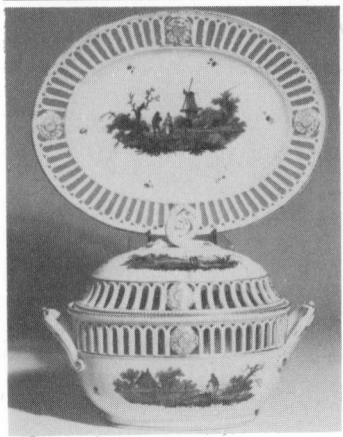

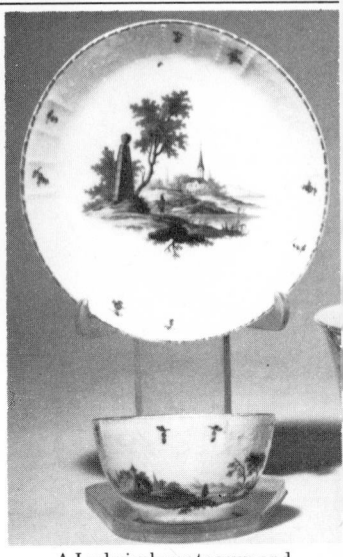

An Oude Loosdrecht two handled pot pourri bowl, cover and stand, painted at Amstel with Dutch figures in river landscapes, windmills and buildings, the borders enriched with gilding, incised M.O.L./y and blue script Amstel mark, the porcelain c. 1780, the decoration somewhat later, the stand 29 cm. wide. **£1,000-1,200**

A Ludwigsburg teacup and saucer, within moulded borders of C and foliage scrolls, and with gilt rims, blue crowned interlaced C's, c. 1765. **£400-450**

Right
A Ludwigsburg figure of a putto, minor chip to his cap, blue interlaced C mark, impressed T3W and 50, c. 1765, 10 cm. high. **£200-300**

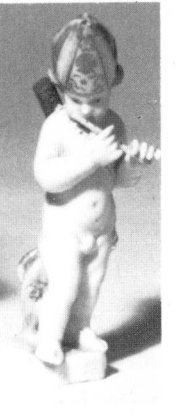

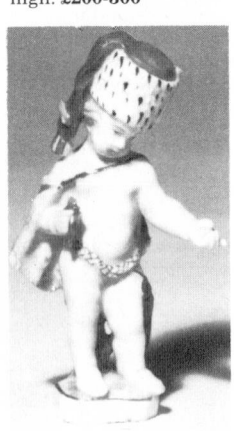

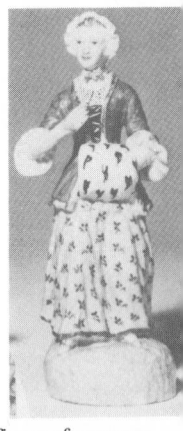

A Ludwigsburg figure of a putto, on shaped square base, repair to head, blue interlaced C mark, incised FF 3 W, c. 1765, 9.5 cm. high. **£180-250**

A Limbach figure of a woman, emblematic of 'Winter', in white, brown and puce, minor chips, purple LB monogram on base, 18 cm. high, c. 1780. **£550-700**
The mark of this factory, which closely resembles Marcolini Meissen, is often confused with it This is of course a much rarer factory, although generally of much poorer quality.

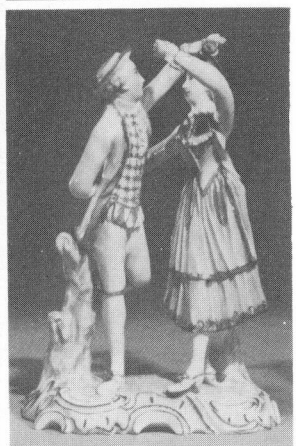

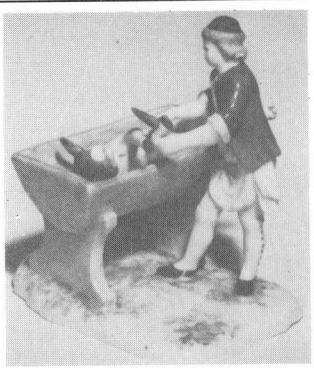

A Ludwigsburg figure of a butcher about to cut up a pig, in iron-red, yellow and black, restored, blue crowned interlaced C mark and incised CS, c. 1765, 11.5 cm. wide. **£500-£600**

A Ludwigsburg group of dancers, modelled by J. Nees, their clothes in iron-red, blue, pink and puce, on puce rococo scroll base, her hat restored, blue crowned interlaced C marks and incised Former's marks and painter's mark, perhaps of Grothe, c. 1765, 16 cm. high. **£1,000-1,200**
Note the somewhat elongated form which is characteristic of this modeller.

LUDWIGSBURG

- porcelain factory was founded in 1758
- J. J. Ringler directed the factory from 1759-99
- best period was from 1765-75
- porcelain has a greyish tone
- specialised in producing figures
- most desirable are the 'Venetian fair groups' produced by Jean-Jacob Louis
- in 1770's figures of a more classical nature were produced
- the later figures were of a much poorer quality
- the factory closed in 1824

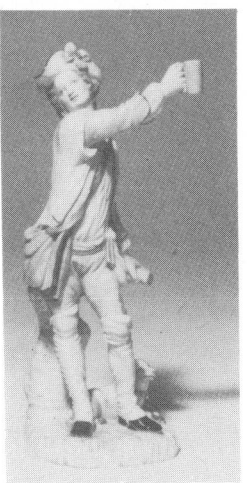

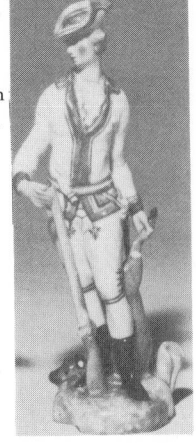

Right
A Ludwigsburg figure of a huntsman, in puce, green and yellow, on grassy mound base, chip to sword, leg of deer lacking, blue interlaced C mark, c. 1765, 16.5 cm. high. **£900-1,000**

A Ludwigsburg figure of a young man, in yellow, white, pink and brown, restoration to his right hand, tankard, hat, left knee and with minor chips, blue crowned interlaced C mark, c. 1765, 15.5 cm. high. **£600-700**

LUDWIGSBURG

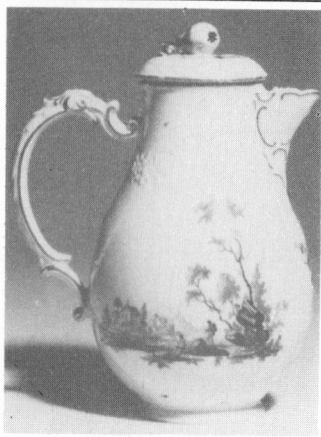

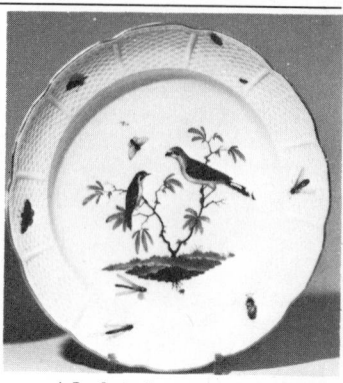

A Ludwigsburg ornithological shaped circular plate, with Ozier moulded border and gilt rim, blue crowned interlaced C mark and impressed RVI, c. 1765, 23 cm. diam. **£200-250**

A Ludwigsburg hot milk jug and cover with pear finial, the scrolling bird's-head handle and scroll-moulded spout enriched with gilding, finial chipped, blue crowned interlaced C mark and Pressnummer 32, c. 1765, 14 cm. high. **£700-900**

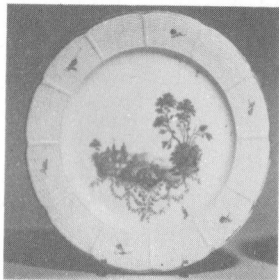

A pair of Ludwigsburg plates, painted with figures and a figure on horseback in river landscapes, blue crowned interlaced C marks, incised RIC, c. 1765, one with minor foot rim chip, 24 cm. diam. **£700-900**

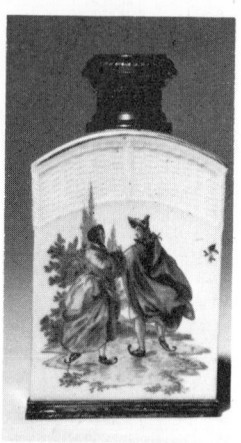

A Ludwigsburg arched rectangular teacaddy, with Ozier border, with later Paris silver-gilt foot rim, neck and stopper, c. 1765, 12.5 cm. high. **£350-450**

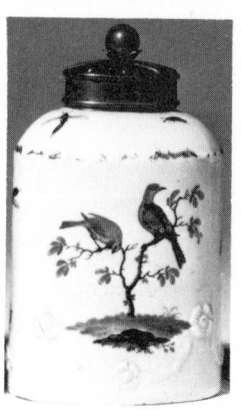

A Ludwigsburg oval teacaddy, moulded with rosettes, painted with birds and butterflies, the shoulder with gilt feuille-de-choux, metal cover, various impressed marks, c. 1770, 13.5 cm. high. **£180-220**

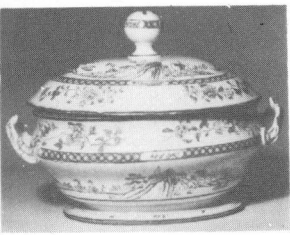

A Ludwigsburg two-handled
oval soup tureen and cover,
painted en grisaille with
Chinoiserie figures, pagodas and
boats, the rococo scroll handles
enriched with gilding, minute
rim chips to cover, impressed
marks I P 3 & 4, c. 1760, 38 cm.
wide. **£700-900**
*The Chinoiserie design, using
cell-diaper friezes, is based on
Chinese exportware designs of the
Yongzheng period (1723-35).*

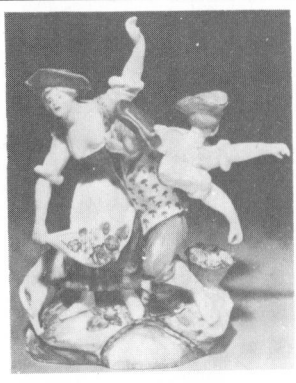

A Marieburg porcelain group of
three figures, their clothes in
colours, on grey rockwork base,
restorations to two arms, marked
with three dots in blue, 1777-78,
9 cm. high. **£500-800**

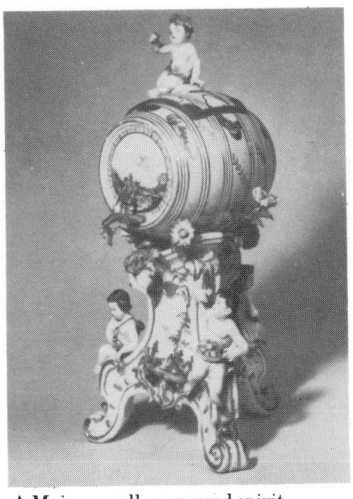

A Meissen yellow ground spirit
barrel on shaped triangular
stand, the ends painted with
hunting scenes, the sides with
lesser panels of porcelain in
colours and camaieu rose, the
yellow grounds with gilt ribs and
foliage, the stand and cover with
four putti emblematic of the
Seasons, with Louis XV ormolu
branches set with flowers
between barrel and stand, some
restoration, blue crossed swords
mark, c. 1745, 45 cm. high.
£1,000-1,500

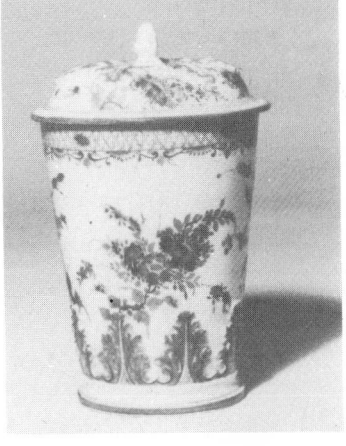

A Böttger flaring beaker and
domed cover, painted in the
Kakiemon palette with scrolling,
flowering chrysanthemum,
enriched in gilding, below a band
of iron-red cell-pattern enclosing
flowerheads, repair to finial,
c. 1722, 15.5 cm. high. **£1,900-
£2,500**
*Both the bucket form and the
acanthus moulding are features
characteristic of Böttger/early
Meissen porcelain, which also
has a slightly creamy appearance,
in contrast to the more bluish
look of later Meissen.*

MEISSEN

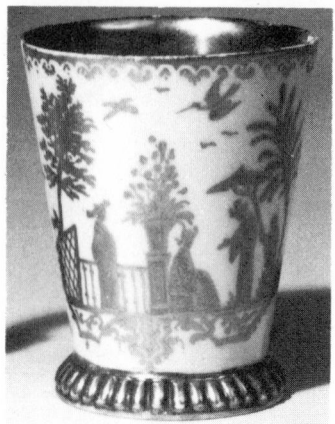

A Meissen Goldchinesen beaker, the interior entirely gilt, rim chips, c. 1725, 8 cm. high. **£550-£750**

A Meissen Chinoiserie octagonal beaker, painted by J. G. Herold beneath a band of gilt Laub-und-Bandelwerk, the interior with a spray of flowers, minute rim chips, blue crossed swords mark within a double circle, c. 1730. **£550-650**

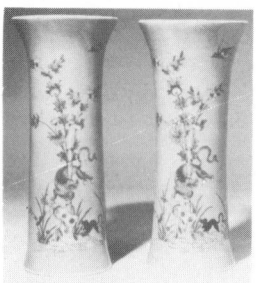

A pair of Meissen pale lilac ground beakers, reserved in Böttger-lustre and other colours with turquoise ch'i-lins, one vase with rim chip, blue caduceus marks, c. 1730, 30 cm. high. **£3,500-4,500**

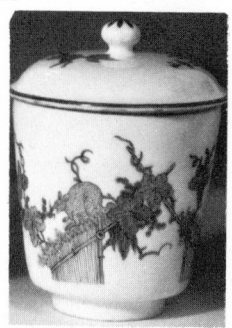

A Meissen Kakiemon beaker and cover, painted with the 'Flying Fox' pattern, with contemporary silver gilt hinge, blue crossed swords mark, c. 1735. **£250-350**

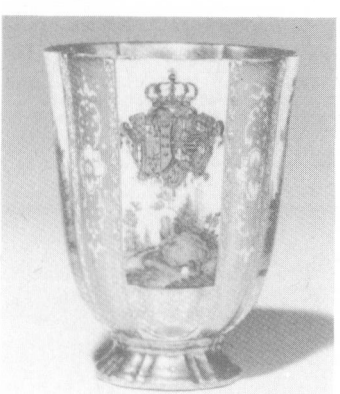

A very rare Meissen armorial beaker, of octafoil section, painted in Kupfergrün with Watteauesque vignettes, one side with the crowned Allianzwappen of Bourbon Palmer and Saxony with the Golden Fleece and the Polish Order of the White, crack in side and chip to foot, blue crossed swords mark, c. 1740, fitted tooled morocco case. **£6,000-£8,000**

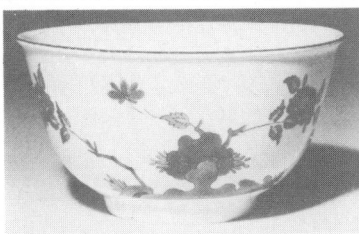

A Meissen Kakiemon circular slop bowl, blue crossed swords and Pressnummer 3, 1730-35, 17 cm. diam. **£800-1,200**

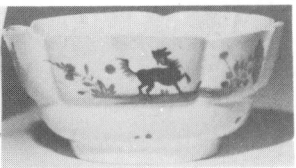

A Meissen bowl, each side painted in the manner of A. F. von Löwenfinck with fabeltière in landscape vignettes, the interior with a flower spray, 1730-35, 23 cm. diam. **£1,100-£1,300**

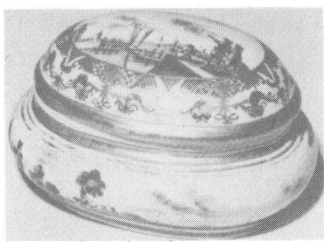

A Meissen KPM oval sugar bowl and cover, painted in the manner of B. G. Hauer with figures in a continuous mountainous river landscape, blue KPM and crossed swords marks, Gilder's mark 88 to both pieces, c. 1725, 13 cm. wide. **£1,500-1,800**

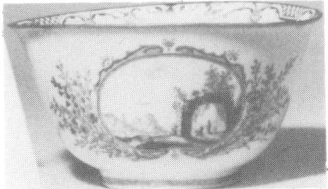

A Meissen Hausmalerei bowl painted en camaieu rose, the interior with a flower spray, the border with gilt scrolls and foliage enclosing trellis pattern panels, minor rim repair, blue crossed swords mark, c. 1750, 18 cm. diam. **£450-550**

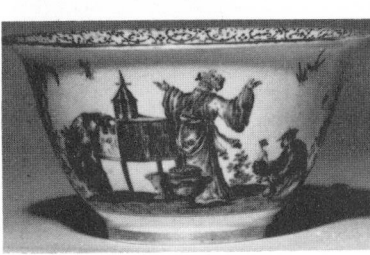

A Meissen Chinoiserie slop bowl, painted with seven large figures, with gilt scroll pattern to the interior, gilt 28 mark, c. 1725, 17 cm. diam. **£1,000-1,500**

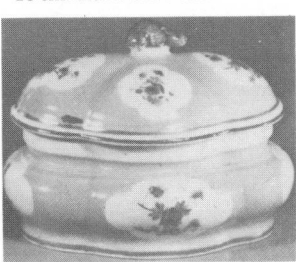

A Meissen celadon ground sugar bowl and cover, decorated in the Kakiemon style with flowering plants in quatrefoil reserves, the cover with coloured rabbit finial and with chocolate rim, blue crossed swords mark, c. 1732. **£7,000-9,000**
The rarity of the celadon ground is reflected in the price

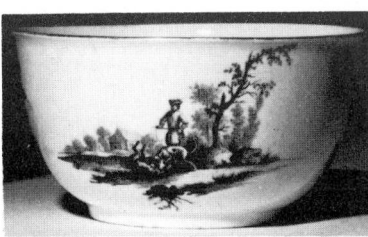

A Meissen slop bowl, from a Jagd service, painted en camaieu rose, with gilt rim, blue crossed swords and dot mark, c. 1770, 16.5 cm. diam. **£400-500**
Probably inspired by prints by Johann Elias Ridinger.

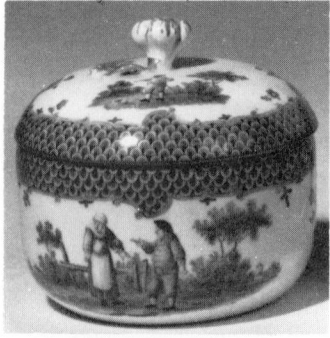

A Meissen circular sugar bowl and domed cover, painted with Teniers figures beneath shaped bands of puce scale pattern, blue crossed swords mark, Pressnummer 53, c. 1750, 11 cm. diam. **£500-700**

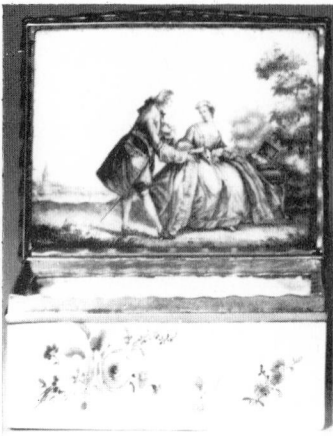

A Meissen gold-mounted snuff box, painted with scattered sprays of deutsche Blumen, the interior of the cover painted en camaieu rose with a gallant and companion, the waved mounts with bracket thumbpiece, c. 1745, 7 cm. wide. **£800-1,000**

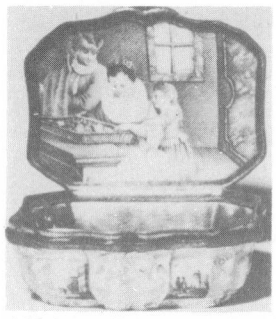

A Meissen silver mounted snuff box and cover, painted with merchants and a camel in an extensive river landscape with trading vessels, the interior to the cover stippled and painted with three figures, c. 1740, cover cracked, 7.5 cm. wide. **£600-800**

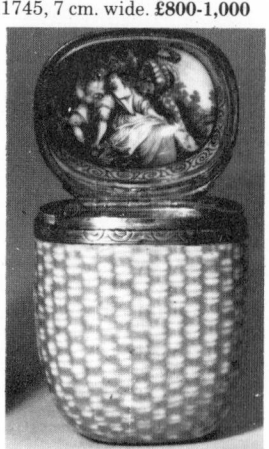

A Meissen snuff box, with hinged silver-gilt mounts, the interior of the cover painted with Harlequin surprising lovers, the exterior moulded with basket weave and rope ties covered in a pale café-au-lait glaze, minute chips to cover, c. 1750, 6.5 cm. high. **£1,000-1,500**

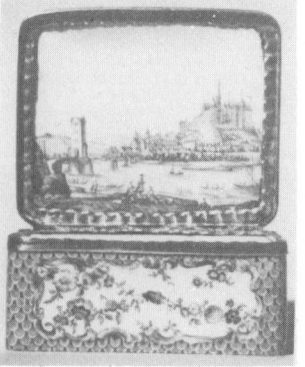

Left
A Meissen silver-gilt mounted snuff box and cover, the interior to the cover painted with a view of the Albrechtsburg, c. 1755, one corner restored, 8.5 cm. wide. **£1,200-1,500**

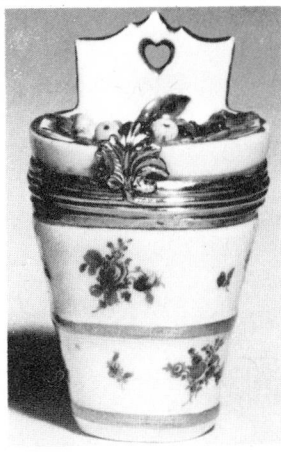

A Meissen snuff box and cover, modelled as a basket of fruit, painted with scattered flowers between gilt lines, c. 1760, 7 cm. high. **£700-1,000**

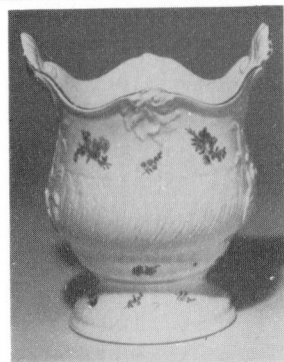

A pair of Meissen two-handled cache pots with shell and foliage moulded handles, with gilt rim, on flaring foot, blue crossed swords marks, c. 1750, 24 cm. high. **£700-900**

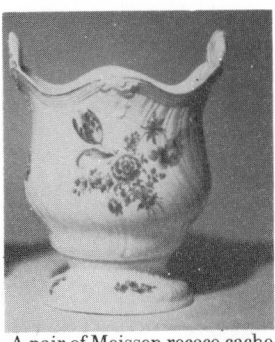

A pair of Meissen rococo cache pots, painted with sprays of deutsche Blumen on a spirally moulded Ozier ground, minor chips to foot rims, blue crossed swords marks, c. 1760, 25 cm. high. **£1,000-1,300**

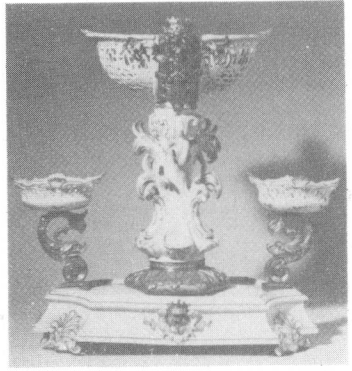

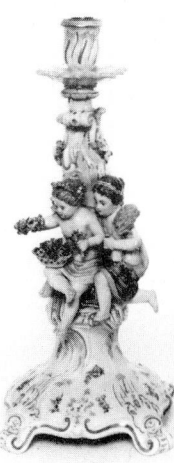

A Meissen armorial ormolu-mounted table centrepiece, the Sulkowski Ozier border of the base applied with the Royal Polish-Saxon coat-of-arms on two sides, enriched in gilt and turquoise, painted with flower sprays in the Kakiemon palette, minor chip repairs, blue crossed swords mark under base, probably late 19th C., 54 cm. high. **£650-950**

Right
Two Meissen candlesticks, each scrolled stem applied with flowers and the figures of two children representing Spring and Summer, painted with scattered flowers, the details gilt, chips, 33 cm., crossed swords in underglaze-blue, incised E128, c. 1900. **£300-500**

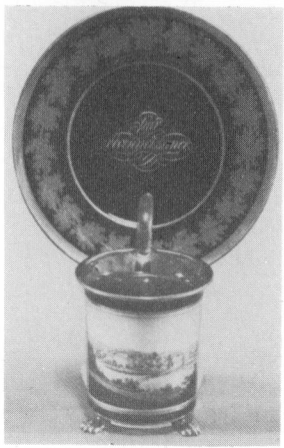

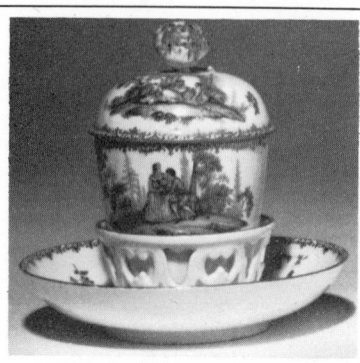

A pair of Meissen chocolate cups, covers and trembleuse saucers, painted with lovers in landscapes, the galleried saucers painted with bouquets of deutsche Blumen, blue crossed swords marks, painter's marks 35, c. 1745. **£900-1,200**

A Meissen Empire cabinet cup and saucer, the cup with buildings in a landscape, all against a blue ground, enriched with gilt, the saucer inscribed 'Par réconnaissance', c. 1820. **£600-800**

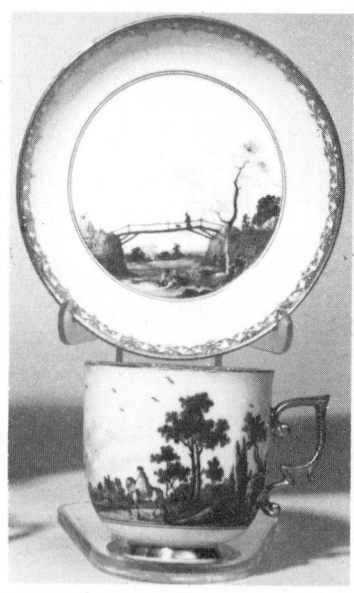

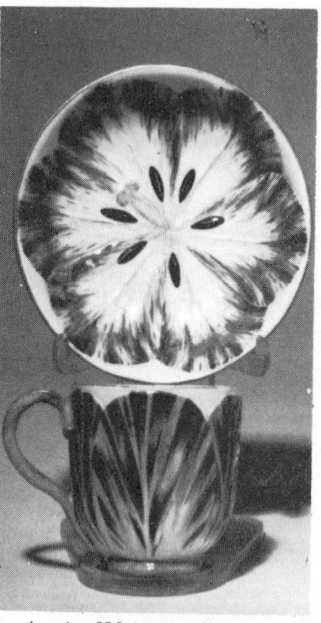

A pair of Meissen coffee cups and saucers, blue crossed swords and gilt 52 marks, the saucers with Pressnummern, c. 1740. **£1,900-£2,200**

A pair of Meissen coffee cups and saucers, moulded with tulip petals painted in puce, yellow and green, the rims enriched with gilding, both saucers with a minute rim chip, blue crossed swords marks, the saucers with Pressnummer 63, c. 1740. **£1,000-1,200**

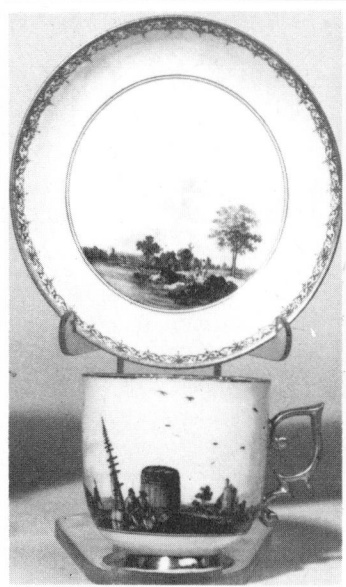

A Meissen coffee cup and saucer, blue crossed swords and gilt 52 marks, c. 1740. **£700-900**

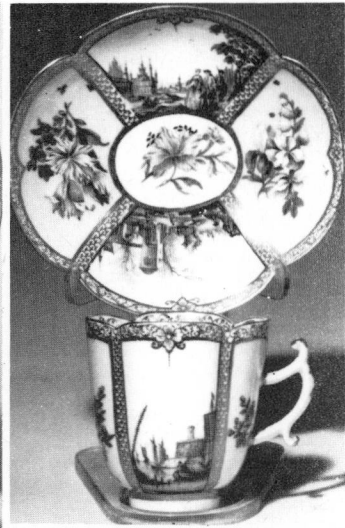

A pair of Meissen yellow ground coffee cups and saucers, painted with harbour scenes, fishing vessels, figures in a river landscape, figures skating in a winter landscape with buildings and courtiers before palaces, blue crossed swords marks, gilder's mark M to each piece, c. 1742. **£2,500-3,000**

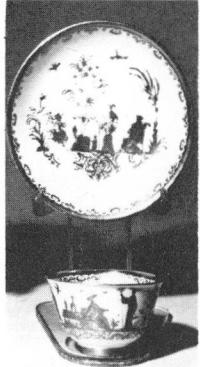

An early Meissen gold Chinese teabowl and saucer, painted with Chinoiserie figures, among flowering plants, within borders of scrolls, the interior of the teabowl with a bird, c. 1723. **£500-800**

A Meissen Chinoiserie teabowl and saucer, painted by J. G. Herold with Chinamen, within oval panels painted with Böttger-lustre and with iron-red foliage, the border with gilt Laub-und-Bandelwerk, gilder's number 44, 1725-28. **£2,000-£2,500**

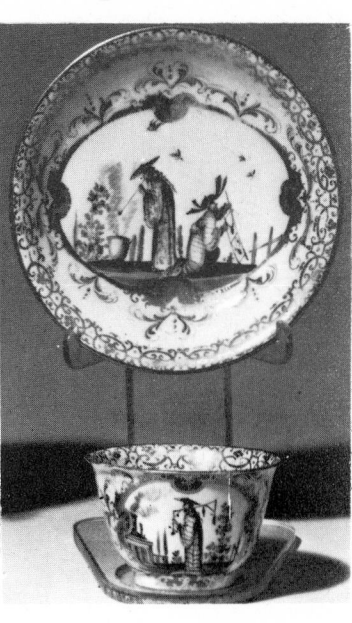

MEISSEN

MEISSEN

- in 1709, J. F. Böttger produced a white hard-paste porcelain
- wares often decorated by outside decorators (Hausmaler)
- in 1720, kilnmaster Stozel came back to Meissen bringing with him J. G. Herold
- from this time Meissen was supreme in enamelling hard-paste porcelain
- crossed swords factory mark started in 1723
- many port scenes painted by C. F. Herold
- finest Meissen figures modelled by J. J. Kändler from 1731
- cut-flower decoration (Schnittblumen) often associated with J. G. Klinger
- from 1755 the rococo style became very popular, especially as a base for figures
- this period saw softer colours used with a great deal of gilding

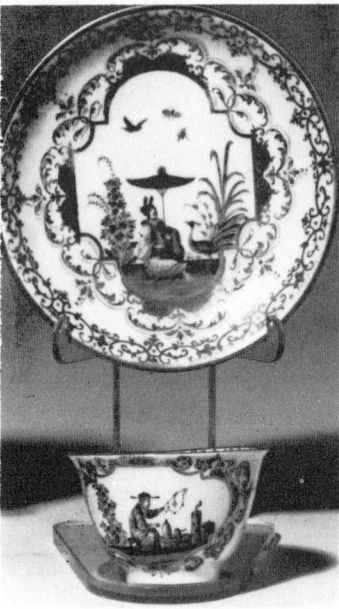

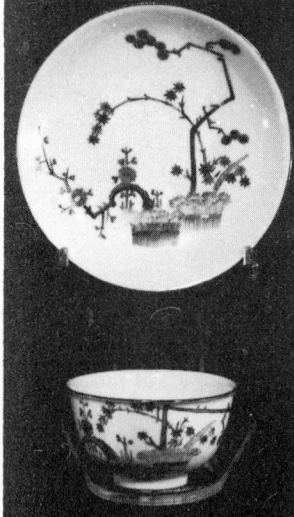

A Meissen Chinoiserie teabowl and saucer, painted, probably by P. E. Schindler, with Orientals within iron-red, Böttger-lustre and gilt Laub-und-Bandelwerk cartouches, and Laub-und-Bandelwerk rims, the interior to the teabowl with a spray of indianische Blumen, the cup with blue caduceus mark and gilt, 57, c. 1730. **£700-1,000**

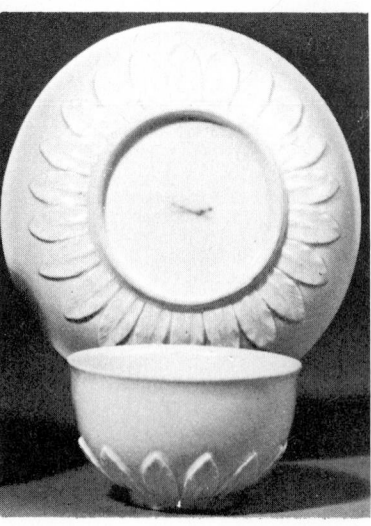

An early Meissen Kakiemon teabowl and saucer, painted with pine, prunus and bamboo, with brown rims, later blue enamel crossed swords mark, Johanneum inventory mark N=2$\frac{+4}{W}$3, c. 1730. **£1,000-1,200**

A pair of Meissen white teabowls and and saucers, minor chips to foot rims of saucers, blue crossed swords marks, c. 1735. **£250-300**

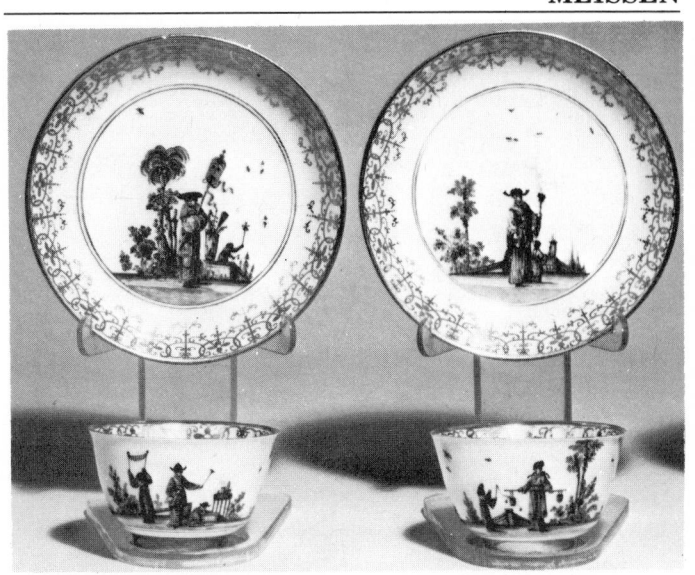

A pair of Meissen Chinoiserie teabowls and saucers, painted by C. F. Herold, with numerous figures on terraces with children, blue crossed swords and gilt H marks, the saucers with Pressnummer 17, c. 1735. **£2,000-2,500**

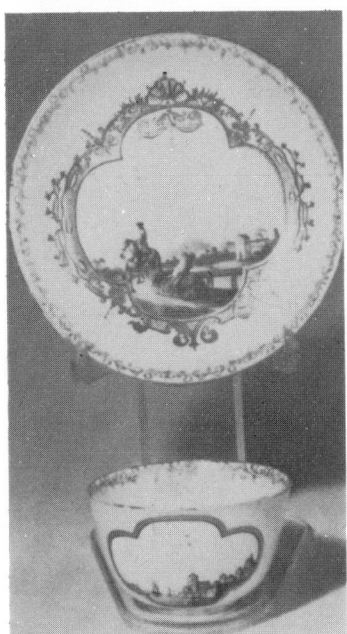

A Meissen yellow-ground teabowl and saucer, painted with a horseman and a riverside town with sailing vessels, blue crossed swords marks and Pressnummern 89 and 2, gilder's mark B . . to each piece, c. 1740. **£600-800**

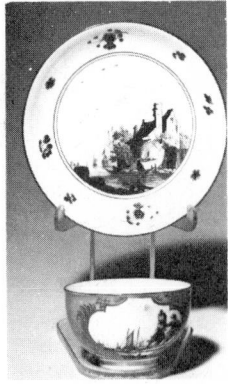

A pair of Meissen pale lilac-ground teabowls and saucers, painted in Schwarzlot with estuary and canal scenes, figures fishing and in boats, within cartouches, enriched in gilt with foliage and Bandelwerk, with chocolate rims, the saucers with scattered flower sprays, blue crossed swords marks, c. 1738, both teabowls and saucers with restorations. **£400-600**

MEISSEN

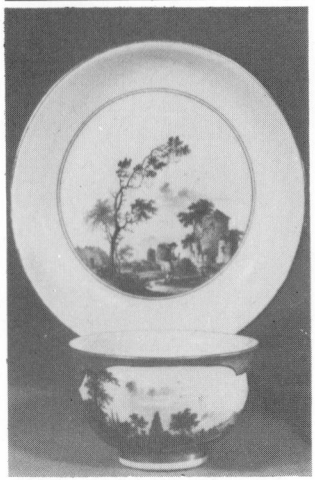

A Meissen iron-red ground teacup and saucer, painted with a man with a pack on his back and a horseman in a river landscape, blue crossed swords marks, c. 1740. **£4,000-5,000**

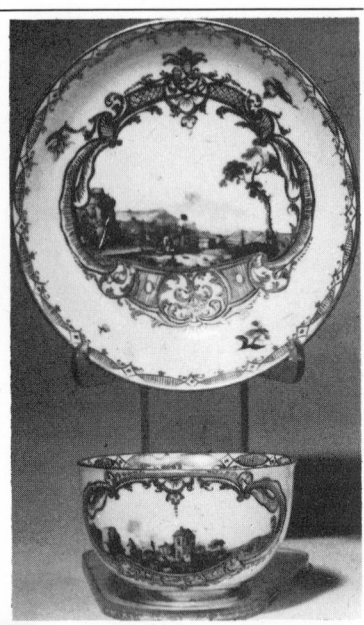

A pair of Meissen teacups and saucers, blue crossed swords marks and gilt 22, various Pressnummern, c. 1742. **£1,900-£2,200**

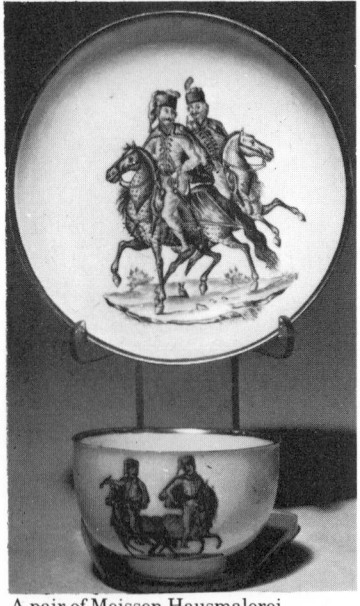

A pair of Meissen Hausmalerei teacups and saucers, painted with equestrian figures in landscape vignettes by F. F. Mayer von Pressnitz, blue crossed swords marks, the saucers with Pressnummer 52, c. 1740. **£2,000-3,000**

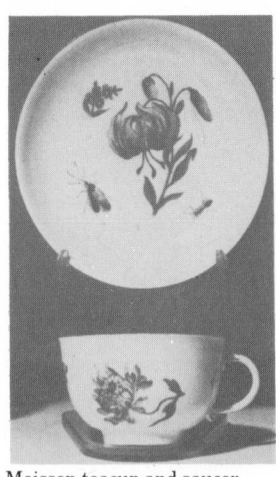

A Meissen teacup and saucer, painted in the manner of Klinger with Holzschnitt Blumen and ombrierte insects, the saucer with a lily, with chocolate rims, blue crossed swords marks, Pressnummer 63, c. 1745. **£550-£750**

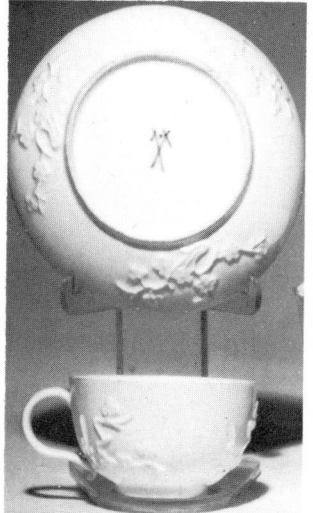

A pair of Meissen white teacups and saucers, the exteriors moulded with sprays of prunus, blue crossed swords and dot marks, c. 1765. **£150-250**

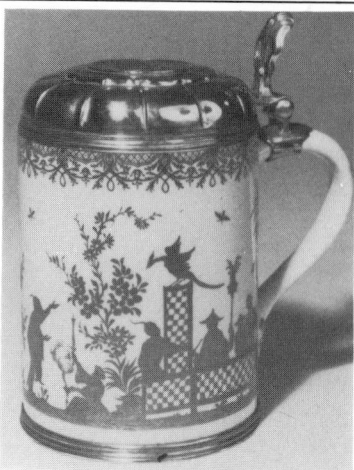

A Meissen gold Chinese cylindrical tankard with silver gilt cover, gilt at Augsburg in the Seuter workshop, the cover inset with a silver medal bust of Count Johann Philip Franz Schönborn, Prince Bishop of Würzburg, blue crossed swords mark, c. 1730. **£5,500-7,500**

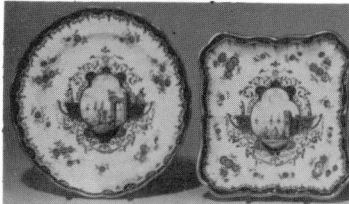

A late Meissen part dessert service, painted in the manner of J. G. Herold, comprising: two shaped square dishes and sixteen plates, one with rim chip. **£2,000-2,500**

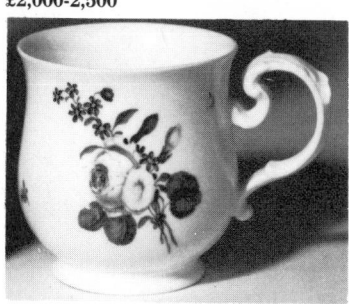

A Meissen baluster mug, painted with scattered deutsche Blumen, after a silver original, blue crossed swords mark, c. 1750, 8 cm. high. **£350-500**

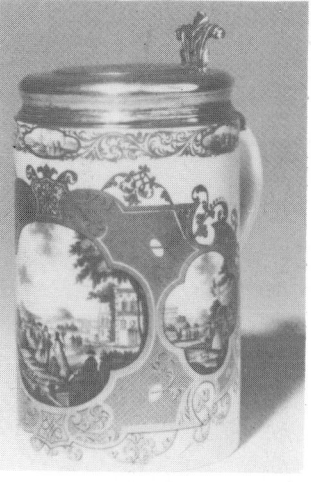

A Meissen cylindrical tankard, painted with three panels in the style of C. F. Herold with court figures, the earlier silver cover with the maker's mark of Claus Borring, Copenhagen, 1707-11, and engraved with a monogram and dated 1743, the porcelain with gilder's mark A, 18.5 cm. high. **£2,500-3,000**

53

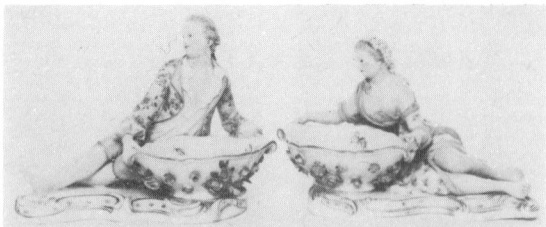

A pair of Meissen sweetmeat dishes, painted with flowers, some damage, 17.5 cm., crossed swords in underglaze-blue, incised 2872 and 2875, late 19th C. **£450-650**

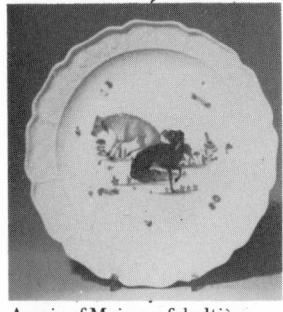

A pair of Meissen fabeltière saucer dishes, with Sulkowski Ozier borders, probably painted by A. F. von Löwenfinck with horned beasts with dappled coats in brown, blue, iron-red, yellow and Böttger-lustre, and with scattered Kakiemon flowers, rim chips, blue crossed swords marks, c. 1735, 25.5 cm. diam. **£1,000-1,400**

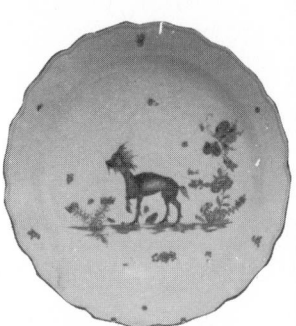

A Meissen fabeltière dish, painted possibly A. F. von Löwenfinck, with a beast between plants, with chocolate rim, blue crossed swords mark and Dreher's mark three incised strokes, 1730-35, 33 cm. diam. **£1,500-2,000**
Since this dish was produced during the period of Löwenfinck's activity at Meissen, it is not impossible that the decoration is by his hand.

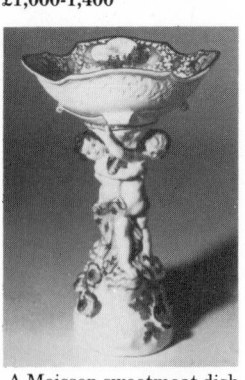

A Meissen sweetmeat dish, modelled by J. J. Kändler, minor chips, traces of blue crossed swords mark on base, Pressnummer 26, 29.5 cm. high, c. 1745. **£1,500-1,800**

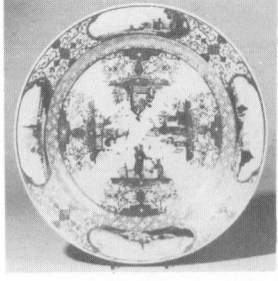

A Meissen Chinoiserie plain circular dish, the centre painted by C. F. Herold, the reverse with scattered indianische Blumen, broken in numerous pieces and repaired, blue crossed swords mark and inscribed H4, c. 1734, 37 cm. diam. **£1,450-1,650**

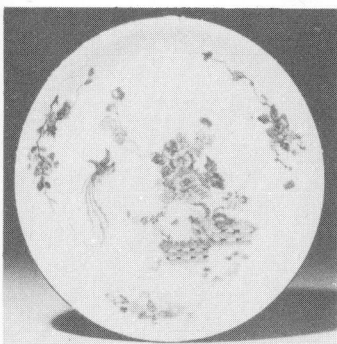

A Meissen saucer dish, painted in Kakiemon style, within a chocolate brown rim, crossed swords mark in underglaze-blue, 22 cm. **£700-800**

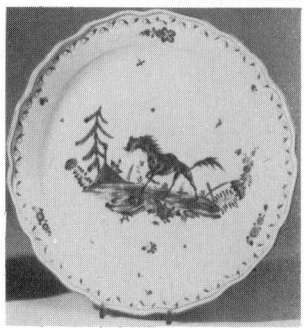

A pair of Meissen fabeltière dishes, painted in the manner of A. F. von Löwenfinck, in puce and gilt, blue crossed swords marks, Pressnummern 20 & 21, c. 1740, 34 cm. diam. **£2,200-£2,600**

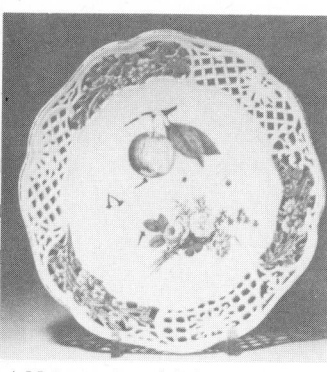

A Meissen pierced dish, painted in colours with fruit and flower sprays, with shaped gilt rim, blue crossed swords mark, Pressnummer 21, c. 1745, 21 cm. diam. **£400-500**

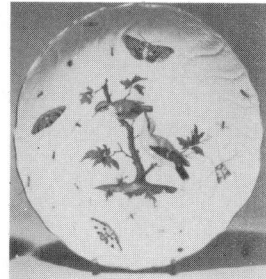

A pair of Meissen ornithological saucer dishes, painted with brightly coloured birds perched on leafy trees and with scattered insects and butterflies, with moulded Ozier borders and with gilt rims, one with two minor rim chips, blue crossed sword marks and Pressnummer 36, c. 1750, 25.5 cm. diam. **£1,000-1,200**

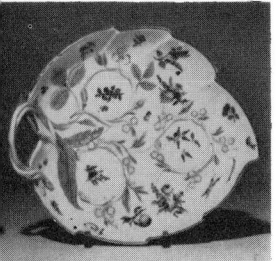

A pair of Meissen leaf-shaped dishes, the foliage moulded to hold three cruets, painted with fruit, vegetables, nuts and flowers, with gilt rims, blue crossed swords marks, c. 1750, 26.5 cm. wide. **£700-900**

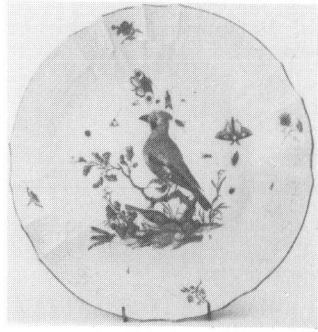

A Meissen dish, crossed swords mark in underglaze-blue, 30 cm., c. 1760. **£660-£760**

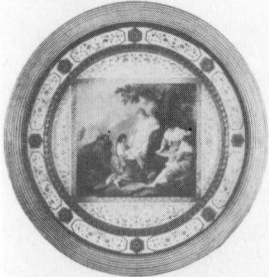

A Meissen wall dish, painted in Vienna style with 'The Finding of Moses' reserved on a polychrome ground with gilt borders and foliate scroll panels, cracked, 42 cm., crossed swords in underglaze-blue, late 19th C., framed. **£300-500**

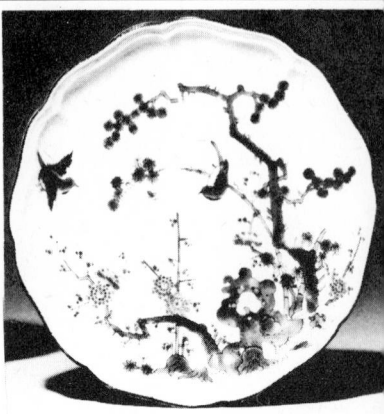

A Meissen saucer, painted in the Kakiemon palette with pine, prunus and bamboo issuing from rockwork, with birds in flight and on branches, enriched in gilding, with chocolate rim, blue crossed swords mark, Pressnummer 24, c. 1740, 14.5 cm. diam. **£400-500**

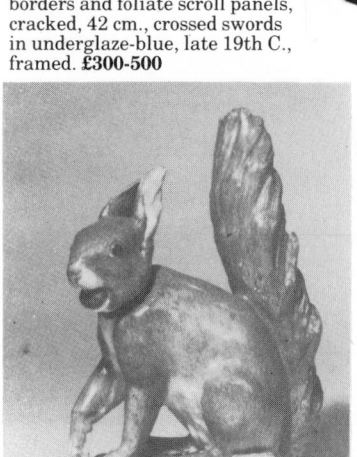

A Meissen figure of a squirrel, modelled by J. J. Kändler, in iron-red and brown fur markings, wearing black collar, a flower encrusted base, repairs to his ears and tail, blue crossed swords mark at back, c. 1740, 22 cm. high. **£1,000-1,500**

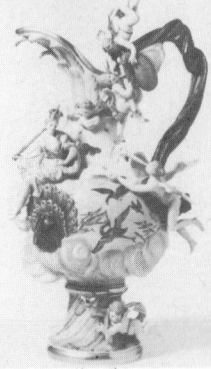

A large Meissen allegorical ewer, after a model by J. J. Kändler, emblematic of 'Air', moulded, applied and brightly coloured with a goddess and playful putti, birds, clouds and feathers, 65 cm., crossed swords in underglaze-blue, incised 327, mid to late 19th C. **£800-1,200**

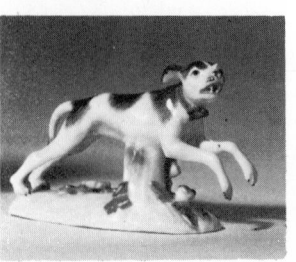

A Meissen figure of a running hound, with puce collar and blue flower buckle, with black markings, one foreleg restored, blue crossed swords mark at back, c. 1745, 10 cm. long. **£300-£400**

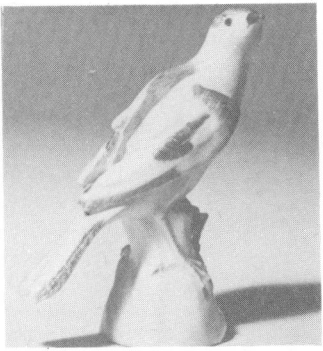

A Meissen figure of a finch, modelled with naturalistic feather markings and coloured in brown and yellow, minor repair to beak, c. 1745, 10.5 cm. high. **£300-400**

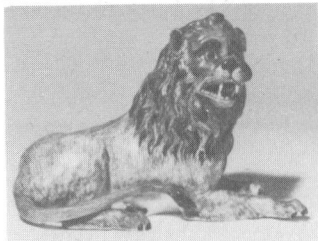

A Meissen figure of a recumbent lion, modelled by J. J. Kändler, moulded and painted with a brown coat, restoration to his right foreleg and tail, one tooth chipped, traces of blue crossed swords mark, Pressnummer 45, c. 1745, 22 cm. wide. **£2,000-£3,000**

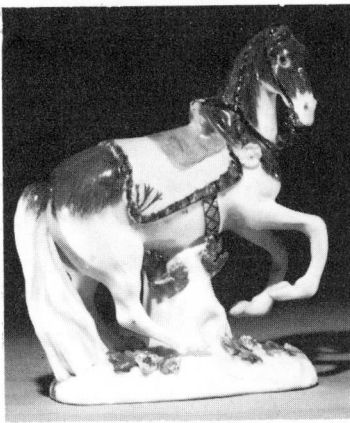

A pair of Meissen figures of horses, modelled by J. J. Kändler, with fur trimmed pink saddle cloths and grey coats to their backs, restorations to forelegs and saddle cloth, blue crossed swords at the back, c. 1745, 11 cm. high. **£600-800**

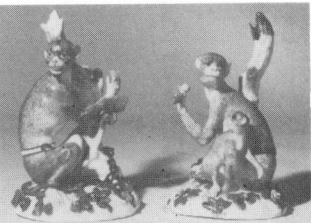

A pair of Meissen figures of monkeys, modelled by J. J. Kändler, decorated in colours, the bases applied with flowers, restoration to hands, top of trees and ear of young monkey, blue crossed swords marks at back, c. 1747, 19 cm. high. **£6,000-£7,000**
Of the figures, animals are by far the most desirable, followed probably by the Commedia dell'Arte and Chinoiserie figures.

A pair of Meissen figures of goats, modelled by J. J. Kändler, he with black patches and she with brown patches, one of his horns chipped, her horns and ears restored, the billy goat with crossed swords mark at back, c. 1745, about 16 cm. long. **£1,000-1,200**

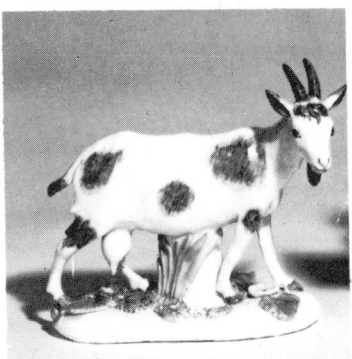

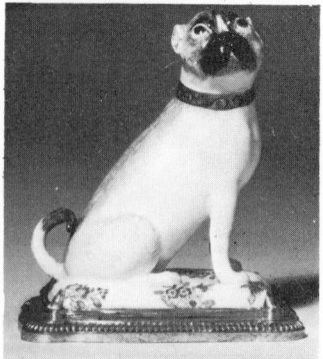

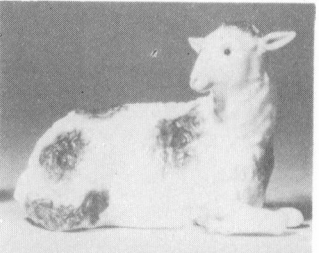

A Meissen figure of a recumbent sheep, modelled by P. J. Reinicke, with moulded fleece and brown black markings, restoration to ears and one foreleg, c. 1750, 17 cm. wide. **£400-600**

A Meissen figure of a seated pug dog, with blue ribbon tied puce collar, the base painted with indianische Blumen, on an ormolu mounted plinth, minor chips to ears, tail restored, blue crossed swords mark, c. 1755, 12.5 cm. high. **£800-1,200**

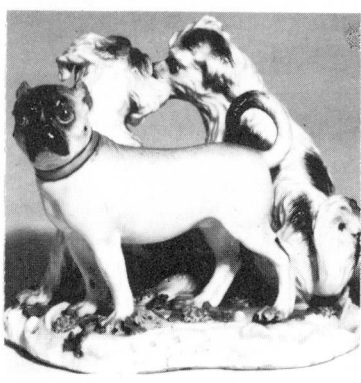

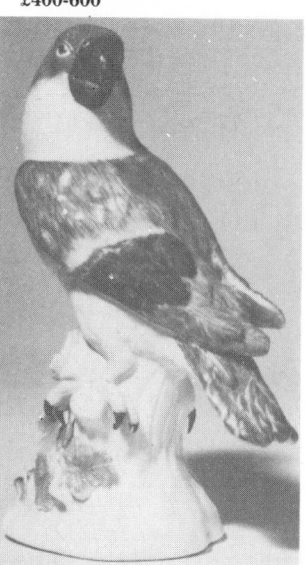

A Meissen canine group of a standing pug and two spaniels, modelled by J. J. Kändler, blue crossed swords mark at back, c. 1750, 17 cm. wide. **£2,000-£3,000**

In animal subjects dogs and horses tend to be the most sought after.

A Meissen figure of a parrot, modelled by J. J. Kändler, with brightly coloured plumage and perched on a tree stump with applied coloured flowers, hair crack in tail feathers, minor chips, blue crossed swords mark, 1745-50, 19 cm. high. **£2,000-£3,000**

A pair of Meissen Bolognese terriers, each with alert expression and a tousled coat in white and grey, 21 cm., one with crossed swords in underglaze-blue, early to mid 19th C., some damage. **£500-700**. If perfect: **£700-1,000**

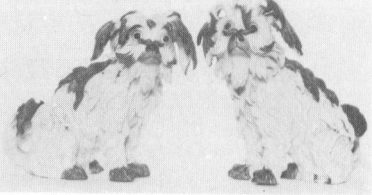

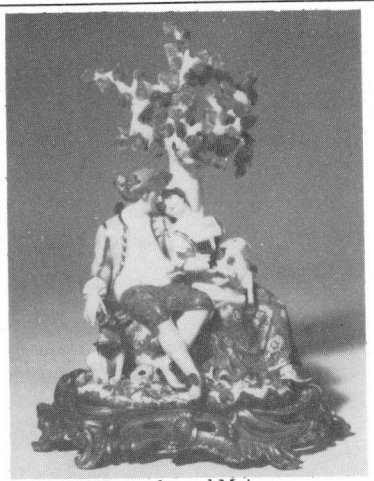

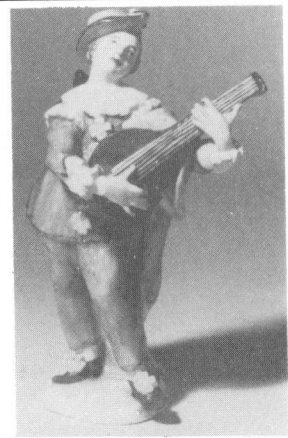

A Louis XV ormolu and Meissen group of seated lovers, modelled by J. J. Kändler, in turquoise, yellow, white, iron-red, pink, black and blue, painted with sprays of Oriental flowers, on a pierced ormolu base with shell, C scrolls and foliage, minor chips and repairs to extremities, c. 1740. £5,000-6,000

A Meissen figure of a lute player, modelled by J. J. Kändler, from the Commedia dell'Arte, in yellow hat, pink cloak, puce jacket and green breeches, repairs to hat, lute and base, 1739-40, 17 cm. high. £2,000-£2,600

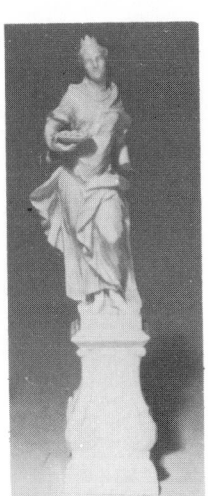

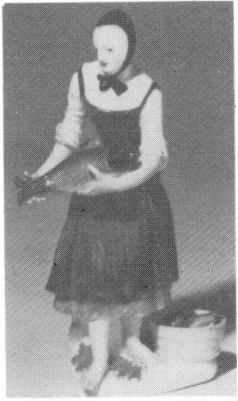

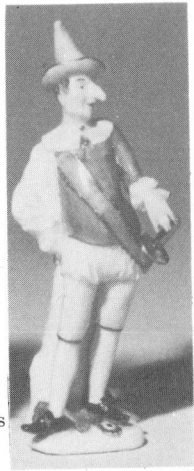

A Meissen figure of a fishwife, modelled by J. J. Kändler, in black cap, brown apron and green skirt, restoration to her arms, hands, feet, the fish and the barrel, blue crossed swords mark at back, c. 1742, 19 cm. high. £800-1,000

A Meissen white figure of a goddess, modelled by J. F. Eberlein, lacks left forearm, c. 1741, 30.5 cm. high. £200-300
From the series of gods and goddesses modelled by Eberlein between 1741 and 1747.

A Meissen figure of a Punchinello, wearing a grey hat, white cloak, yellow breeches and black shoes, his sword held in a pink sash on his green coat, left hand and foliage damaged, blue crossed swords mark at back, c. 1744, 14 cm. high. £8,000-10,000

MEISSEN

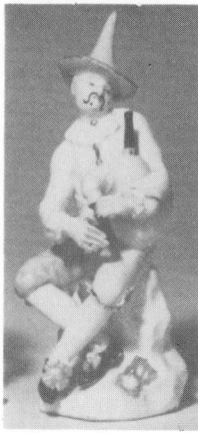

A Meissen figure of Harlequin, in pink hat, white shirt and pink and yellow breeches, restorations to his hat, fingers, left leg and bagpipes, minor chips, blue crossed swords marks at back, c. 1742, 14 cm. high. **£800-1,000**

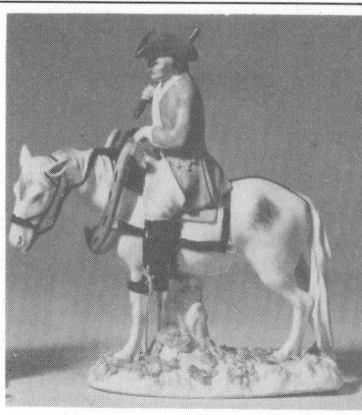

A Meissen equestrian figure of a man, in dark brown tricorn hat, brown jacket, beige breeches and knee length black boots, restored, blue crossed swords mark, c. 1745, 21 cm. wide. **£500-£700**

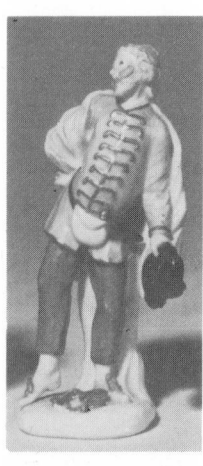

A Meissen figure of Scapin, dressed in yellow cloak, pink coat, blue trousers and yellow shoes, the rockwork base applied with flower sprays, blue crossed swords mark at back, c. 1744, 13 cm. high. **£3,000-4,000**
The Italian comedy (or Commedia dell'Arte) was a favourite subject for porcelain modellers, especially at Meissen and later at Bow and Chelsea.

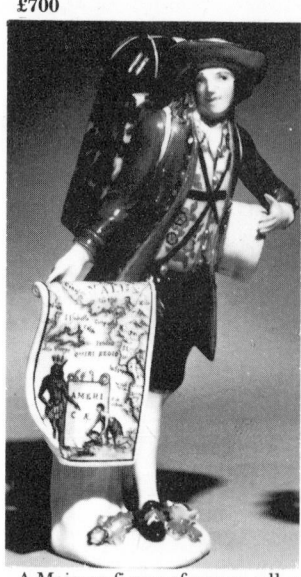

A Meissen figure of a map-seller, modelled by J. J. Kändler, holding a map of America, dressed in iron-red lined blue coat and yellow waistcoat with indianische Blumen and black breeches, restorations to his hat and his left hand, c. 1745, 16.5 cm. high. **£2,000-2,500**
Though this model is frequently found holding maps of Europe, no comparable American map is recorded.

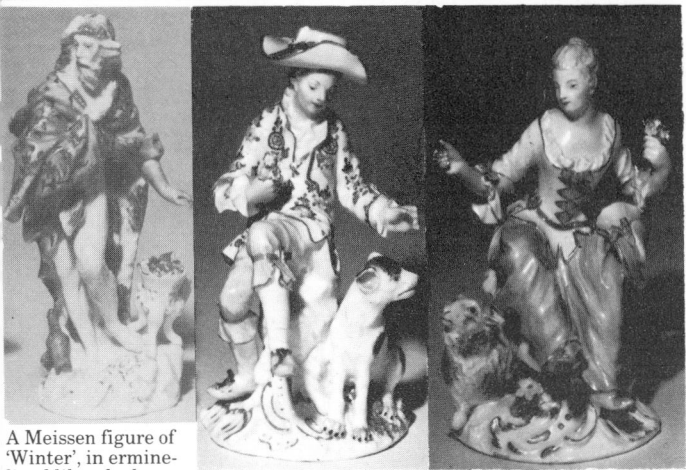

A Meissen figure of 'Winter', in ermine-lined lilac cloak painted with flowers in puce and gilt and standing beside a brazier and with a green bottle at his feet, chips to left arm restored, blue crossed swords mark at back, c. 1745, 14 cm. high. **£200-£300**

A pair of Meissen figures of a shepherd and shepherdess, in yellow, white and puce, her left arm re-stuck, minor chips, blue crossed swords marks at back, c. 1745, 16 cm. high. **£1,000-1,200**

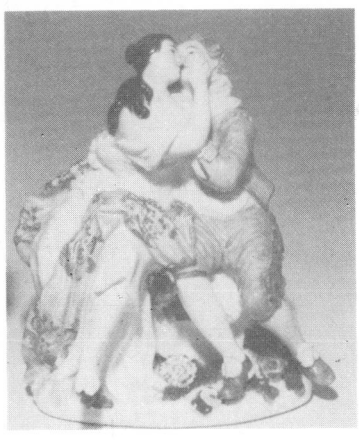

A Meissen group of seated lovers, modelled by J. F. Eberlein, in pink jacket, turquoise breeches, puce ruffs and white dress with pink flowered cloak, restoration to her right arm and left leg, his left leg and right foot, base cracked, c. 1745, 15.5 cm. high. **£1,000-£1,200**

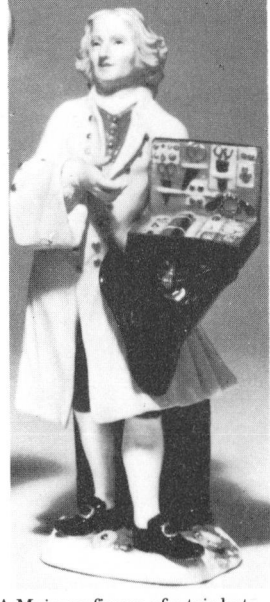

A Meissen figure of a trinket-seller from the large 'Cris de Paris' series, in white coat, blue waistcoat, black breeches and a black tricorn hat, restored, c. 1745, 19 cm. high. **£1,000-£1,200**

MEISSEN

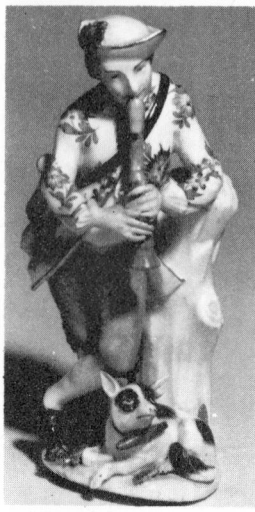

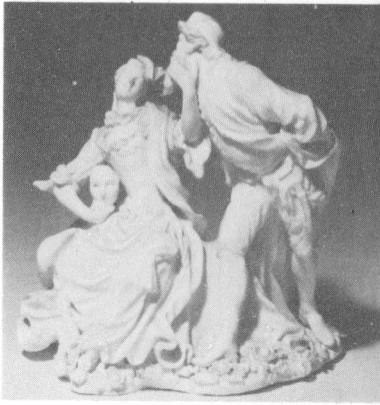

A Meissen white group of
Scaramouche and Columbine,
modelled by J. J. Kändler,
repairs and firing crack through
base, c. 1745, 16.5 cm. high.
£500-700

A Meissen figure of a shepherd
with a dog at his feet, modelled
by J. J. Kändler and P. Reinicke,
in yellow hat, white coat with
indianische Blumen, turquoise
breeches, repair to his fingers,
his instrument and the dog's
collar, blue crossed swords mark
at back, 1748-50, 16 cm. high.
£700-900
This figure was copied at Bow.

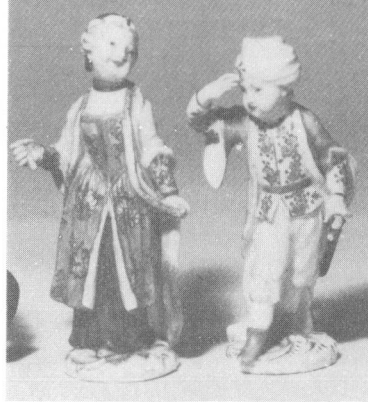

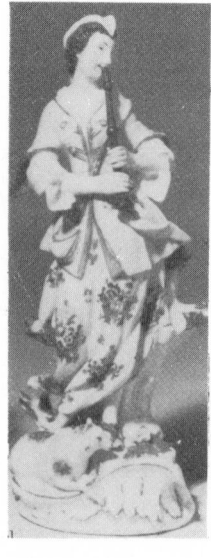

A pair of Meissen figures of
children, in Turkish dress, in
yellow, white, blue and puce,
chips to his left hand and sword,
the top of her fan missing, blue
crossed swords marks, c. 1750,
13 cm. high. **£500-650**

A Meissen figure of a
shepherdess, in a pink-lined
yellow jacket, white shirt and
flower-decorated skirt, on gilt
edged scrolled mound base,
restorations to the clarinet, her
arms and extremities, blue
crossed swords mark at back,
c. 1745, 24.5 cm. high. **£400-600**

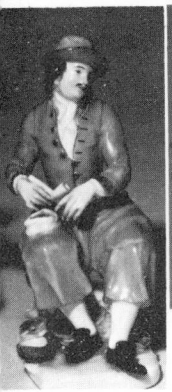

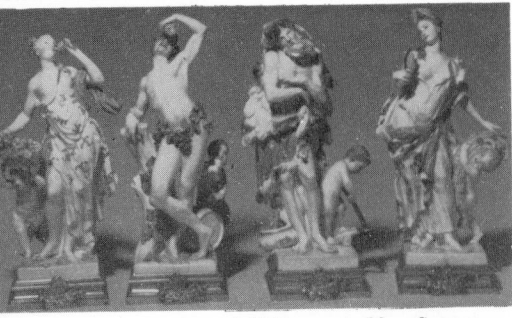

A Meissen figure of a Dutchman, modelled by J. F. Eberlein, in grey and puce hat, brown jacket and trousers, seated on a blue cushion, the end of his pipe chipped, hair crack through wrist, blue crossed swords mark at back, c. 1750, 13 cm. high. **£450-650**
First modelled by Eberlein in 1746.

A Meissen set of four figures emblematic of 'The Seasons', modelled by J. J. Kändler, 'Winter' with hair crack through brazier, 'Spring' with hair crack to base and chips to fingers and flowers, 'Summer' with left arm restuck, crack to base, chips to sickle and fingers, 'Autumn' with crack at waist and base, putto's legs damaged, blue crossed swords marks on base and back, c. 1750, overall height 30 cm. **£5,000-£6,000**

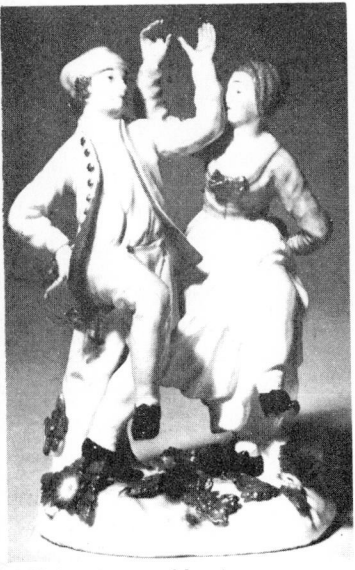

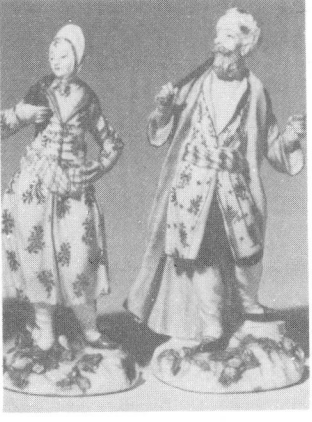

A Meissen group of dancing Dutch peasants, modelled by P. Reinicke, in pale-coloured clothes, blue crossed swords mark at back, c. 1750, minor repair to hands, 14.5 cm. high. **£1,000-1,500**

A pair of Meissen figures of a Bulgar and Persian companion, from a series of Orientals, modelled by J. J. Kändler and P. Reinicke, in puce, pink, cream, gold and blue, his left arm, right sleeve and his staff damaged, blue crossed swords marks at back, c. 1750, 22 cm. high. **£4,000-5,000**
Taken from the engravings by G. Scotin in De Ferriol: 'Receuil de Cent Estampes représentant différentes Nations du Levant', Paris 1714.

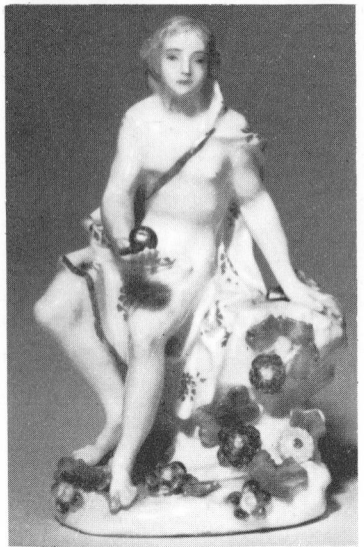

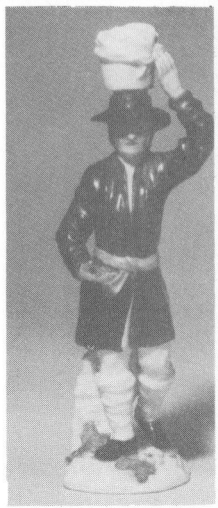

A Meissen figure of Paris, in a white cloak with gilt flowers, the mound base applied with coloured flowers, restoration to his right arm and golden ball, and the fingers of his left hand, minor chip, c. 1755, 12 cm. high. **£300-400**

A Meissen figure of biscuit seller, modelled by J. J. Kändler, in a black hat, brown jacket with a pink sash and white breeches, repair to his hat and right arm, blue crossed swords mark at back, c. 1750, 17 cm. high. **£700-£800**

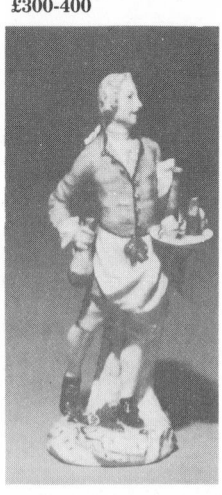

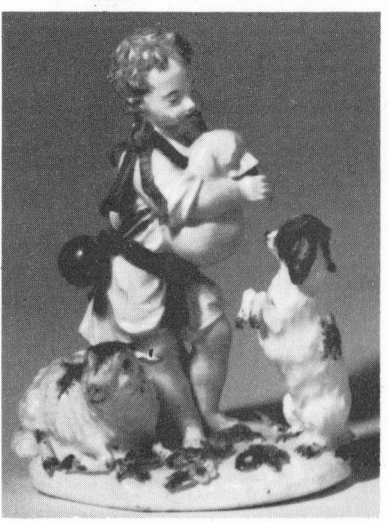

A Meissen figure of a waiter, from the 'Cris de Paris' series, modelled by Kändler and Reinicke, in pink coat and yellow breeches, chip to his bow and to one carafe, blue crossed swords mark at back, Pressnummer 18, c. 1753, 13.5 cm. high. **£1,500-£1,800**

A Meissen group of a young shepherd boy, playing bagpipes with a begging dog at his feet and a recumbent sheep at his side, minor chips, blue crossed swords mark and impressed No. 14, c. 1760, the decoration perhaps later, 14 cm. high. **£450-£650**

MEISSEN

- late 19th C. figures were often disregarded and treated disparingly by dealers
- due to the increased demand and high prices of pieces from 1720-60, later pieces are becoming much more collectable
- the same is true for many of the other great 18th C. factories and is an area where collectors can often find bargains

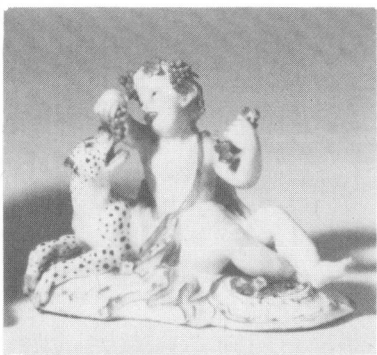

A Meissen figure of the infant Bacchus, draped in a pink and yellow flowered cape, minor chips, c. 1760, 13 cm. wide. **£500-£750**

MEISSEN MARKS

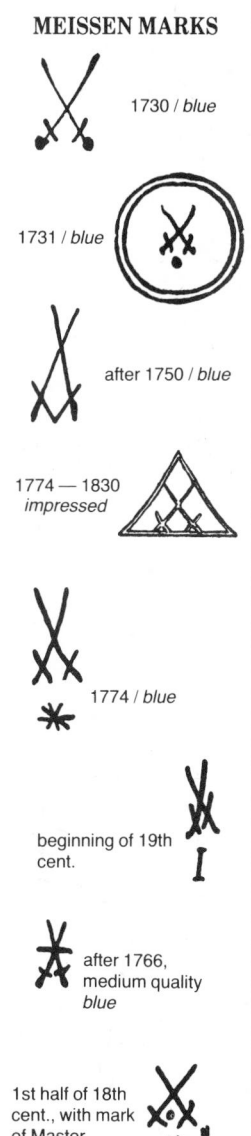

1730 / *blue*

1731 / *blue*

after 1750 / *blue*

1774 — 1830 *impressed*

1774 / *blue*

beginning of 19th cent.

after 1766, medium quality *blue*

1st half of 18th cent., with mark of Master Moebius / *blue*

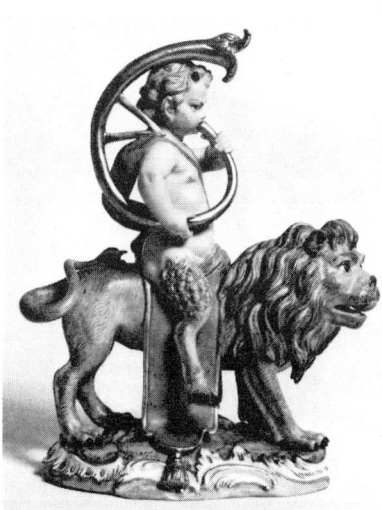

A Meissen figure of a youthful satyr, seated on a lion with an orange saddle cloth and blowing into a large gilt horn, 18.5 cm., crossed swords in underglaze-blue, incised D55, mid 19th C. **£300-400**

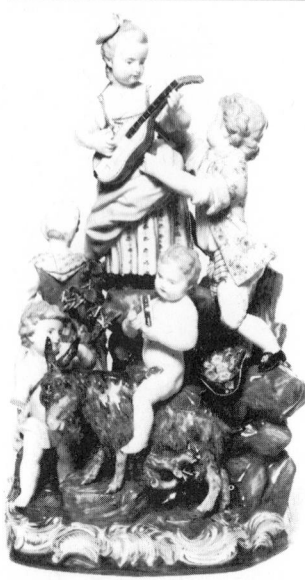

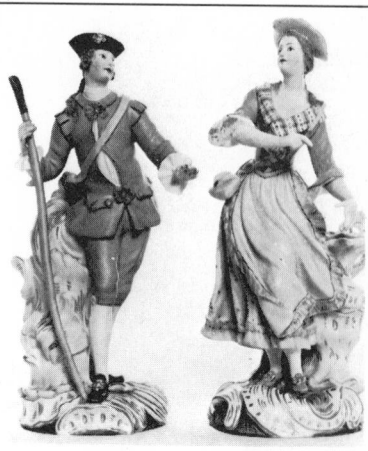

A pair of Meissen figures, the girl with a satchel and apron over a blue jacket and sprigged skirt, her companion wearing a blue jacket and pink breeches, restored, crossed swords in underglaze-blue, incised 1774, 17 and 17.5 cm., late 19th C. **£250-350**

A Meissen festive group, some damage, crossed swords in underglaze-blue, incised C.59 and painted 17 in red, 34 cm., mid 19th C. **£600-700**

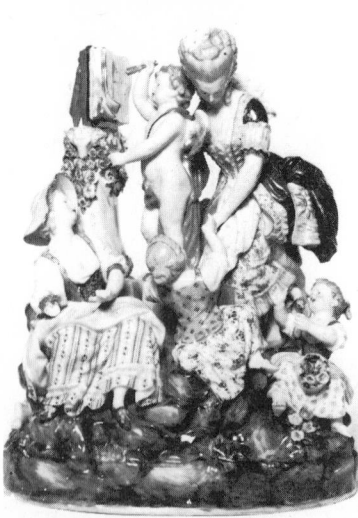

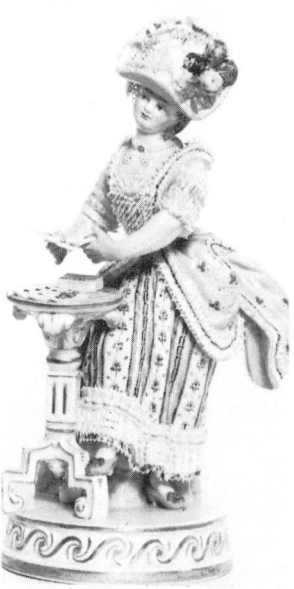

A Meissen group of 'Lessons in Love', after the original model by M. V. Acier, some damage, crossed swords in underglaze-blue, incised F74, painted 17 in red, 29 cm., mid 19th C. **£500-£700**

A Meissen figure of a card player, the young woman wearing a lace edged eighteenth century style dress and robe, some lace missing, crossed swords in underglaze-blue, incised F64, 15.5 cm., late 19th C. **£300-400**

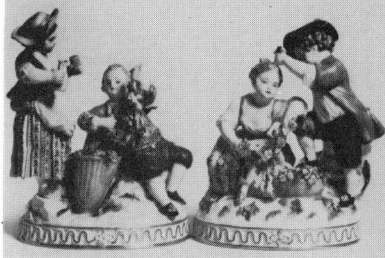

A pair of Meissen groups, each modelled as two rustic children in eighteenth century dress, minor chips, crossed swords in underglaze-blue, incised F92 and F93, 16 and 15 cm., c. 1900. **£450-550**

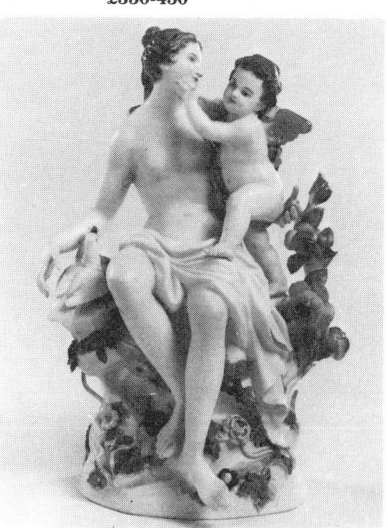

A Meissen group of a shepherd and shepherdess, the girl holding a sheep the man with a dog, chips, crossed swords in underglaze-blue, incised D19, 22.5 cm., mid to late 19th C. **£350-450**

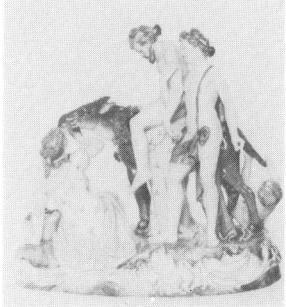

A Meissen Bacchic group, the drunken god supported on the back of an ass by a younger acolyte, the rocky base edged with gilt scrolls, restored, underglaze-blue crossed swords, incised 2724, 21.3 cm., late 19th C. **£200-250**
Figures with classical influence do not generally realise as much as 18th C. style subjects. Compare this group with the Samson interpretation of the Meissen original below.

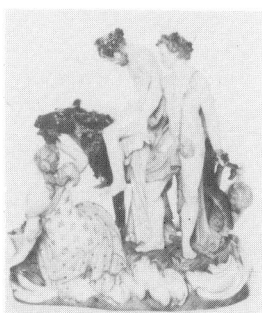

A Meissen group of Venus and Cupid, chips, crossed swords in underglaze-blue, incised 870, 19 cm., late 19th C. **£250-350**

A Samson 'Meissen' Bacchic group, on a mound base edged with gilt scrolls, chips, crossed cross and S in underglaze-blue, 19 cm. late 19th C. **£100-150**

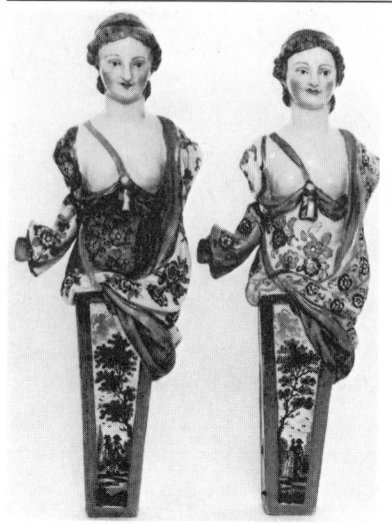

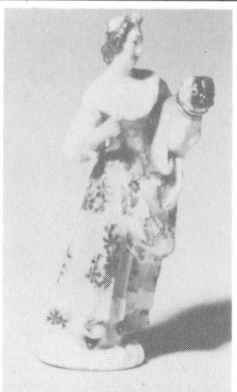

A Meissen scent flask, modelled as a Court figure holding a pug dog in her left arm, the pug dog's head forming the stopper mounted in gilt metal, blue crossed swords mark to base, c. 1750, repair to right hand, 8 cm. high. **£800-1,200**

A pair of Meissen finials, each in the form of a term, each set on a tapering column painted with lovers in gardens and floral sprigs, one with repair to drapery, crossed swords in underglaze-blue, incised G32, late 19th C., 19 cm. **£100-150**

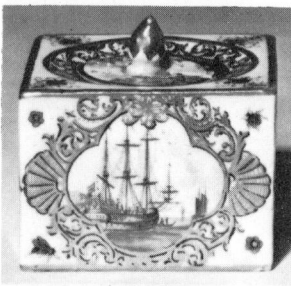

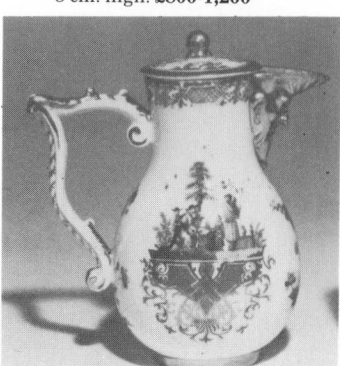

A Meissen square ink pot and cover, the panels to the sides painted with a ship, figures and horsemen, within gilt and chocolate shell and scroll cartouches, cover damaged, traces of blue crossed swords mark, Pressnummer 36, c. 1745, 6.5 cm. square. **£300-400**

A Meissen Chinoiserie hot milk jug and cover, of Clemens August type, painted by C. F. Herold with Chinoiserie figures and children above lustre, gold and iron-red Laub-und-Bandelwerk supports and indianische Blumen, crack in body, restoration to spout and cover, blue crossed swords mark and gilder's number 36, c. 1725, 15 cm. high. **£400-500**

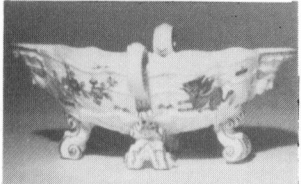

Two Meissen Kakiemon sauceboats, one with rim chip, blue crossed swords marks, Pressnummer 46, one possibly later decorated, c. 1730, 25 cm. wide. **£1,000-1,500**

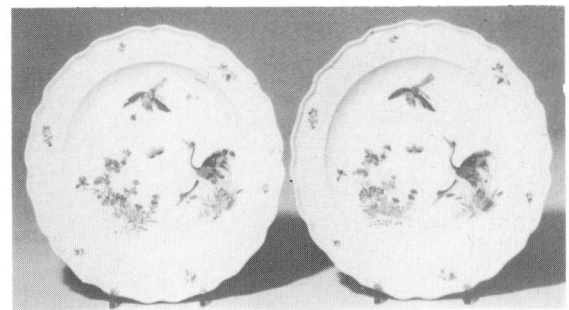

A pair of Meissen Kakiemon plates, with Sulkowski Ozier borders, painted with storks and birds in flight above flowering plants and insects, blue crossed swords marks, c. 1735, 23.5 cm. diam. **£2,000-2,500**

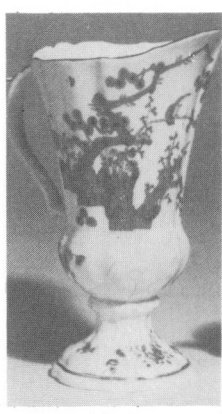

A Meissen Kakiemon milk jug, of fluted form, restored, blue crossed swords mark, c. 1735, 16 cm. high. **£400-500**

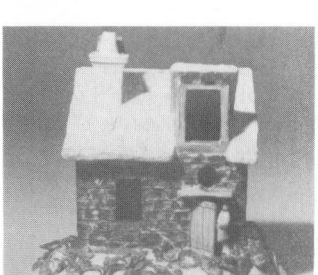

A Meissen model of a cottage, with a figure wearing a black tricorn hat and yellow jacket appearing from a door, minor chips and repairs to foliage, blue crossed swords mark, c. 1745. **£2,500-3,500**

When an inventory was taken of Count Bruhl's effects at the time of his death there were no less than 67 houses of this type in porcelain. They may be attributed to Ehder and Reinicke under the supervision of Kändler.

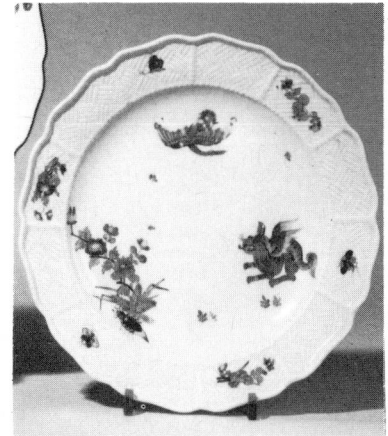

A pair of Meissen Kakiemon plates, painted with storks, ky'lin, insects and flowering plants, within Ozier moulded shaped borders, blue crossed swords mark, c. 1735, 23.5 cm. diam. **£500-700**

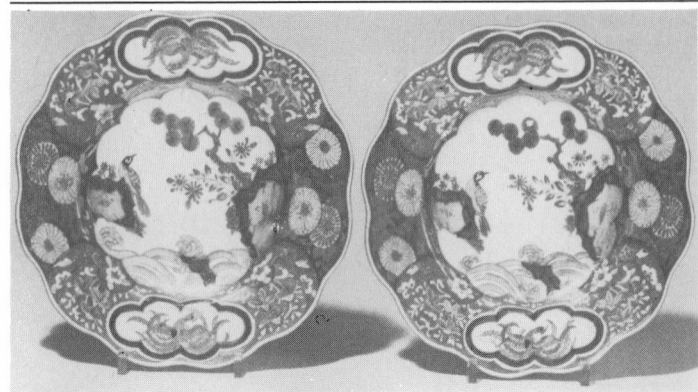

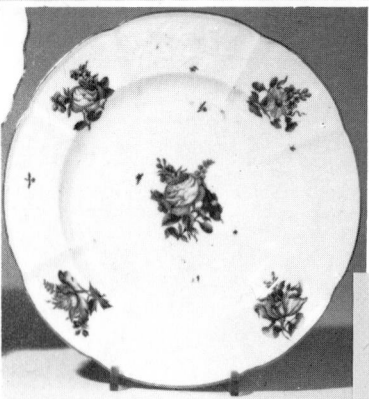

A pair of Meissen brocade pattern plates, with waved gilt rims, blue crossed swords and star mark, Pressnummer 12, c. 1735, 23.5 cm. diam. **£1,000-£1,100**
These are direct copies of the Japanese Imari originals.

A pair of Meissen plates, moulded with Gotzkowsky erhabene Blumen, with gilt rims, minor rim chip repairs, blue crossed swords mark, c. 1745, 24 cm. diam. **£400-500**

One of a pair of Meissen Marcolini plates, one painted with 'Les Albanois d'Athènes', blue crossed swords and star marks and Pressnummer 54, 24 cm. diam., c. 1790. **£1,000-£1,200**

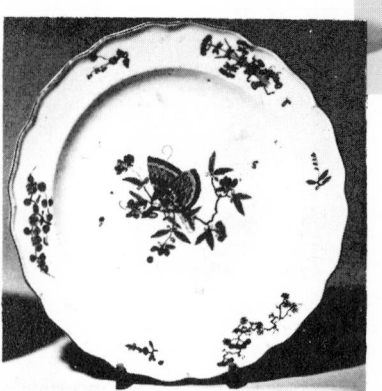

A Meissen plate, painted in the Kakiemon palette with the Schmetterling pattern, with waved chocolate rim, blue crossed swords mark, c. 1735, star crack to base, 23.5 cm. diam. **£140-170**. If perfect: **£500-800**

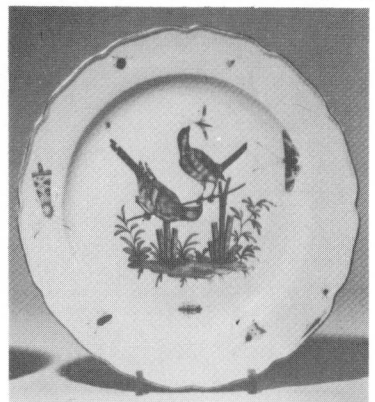

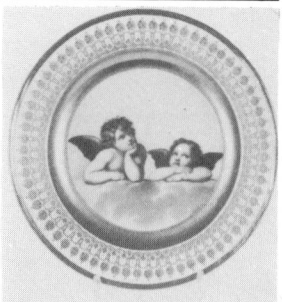

A Meissen cabinet plate, painted after Raphael, crossed swords in underglaze-blue, 24.1 cm. early 19th C. **£200-250**

A pair of Meissen ornithological plates, painted with birds among flowering plants and with scattered insects, with gilt rims, blue crossed swords marks, Pressnummer 36, c. 1745, 23.5 cm. diam. **£600-£800**

Right
A Meissen rococo armorial plate, painted in colours and gilt with 'allianzwappen' within a brown, iron-red, blue, yellow and puce rocaille surround, the Ozier border with sprays of flowers and the rim gilt, blue crossed swords mark and Pressnummer 19, c. 1745, 24 cm. diam. **£800-1,200**

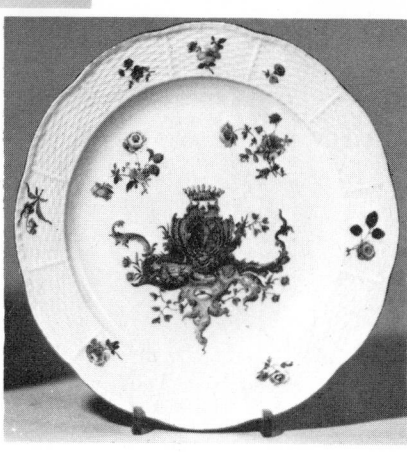

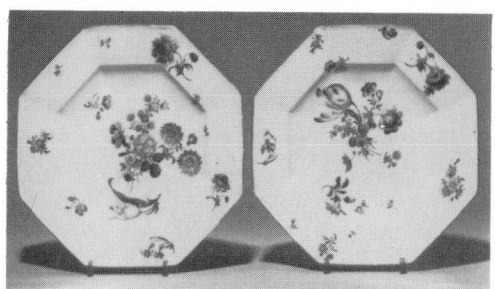

Six Meissen octagonal plates, painted with scattered deutsche Blumen, with gilt rims, blue crossed swords marks, two with Pressnummer 22, c. 1745, 23.5 cm. wide. **£1,100-1,200**

MEISSEN

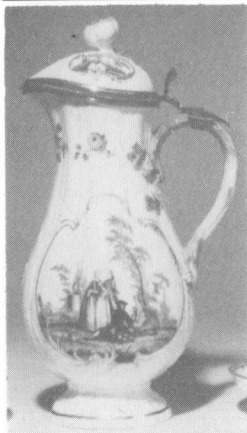

A Meissen chocolate pot and silver gilt mounted beaked cover, painted with lovers in landscapes within gilt scroll cartouches, reserved on a moulded Dulong pattern ground, foot chipped, minor chips to the flowers, blue crossed swords mark, c. 1750, 24.5 cm. high. **£1,100-1,500**

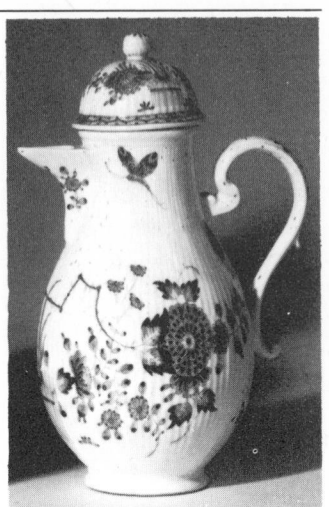

A Meissen baluster coffee pot and cover, moulded with slight flutes and painted en camaieu rose and gilt with chrysanthemum and prunus issuing from hay bales, minor glaze faults, blue crossed swords and dot mark, Pressnummer 67, c. 1770, 24.5 cm. high. **£200-300**
Note the re-emergence of the use of oriental flowers (indianische Blumen), it had become unfashionable in the mid 18th C.

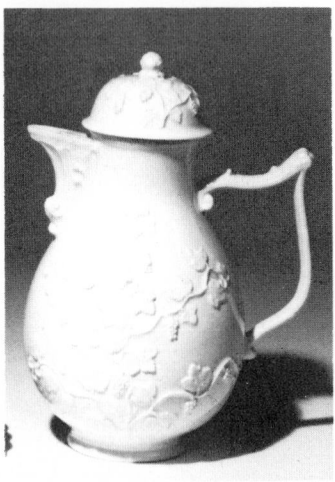

A Meissen white coffee pot and domed cover, moulded with scrolling grapes and vine leaves and with scroll spout, spout chipped, blue crossed swords mark, c. 1745, 22 cm. high. **£400-£600**
Although this has no obvious counterpart in Fujian porcelain, the moulding technique was certainly based on Chinese originals.

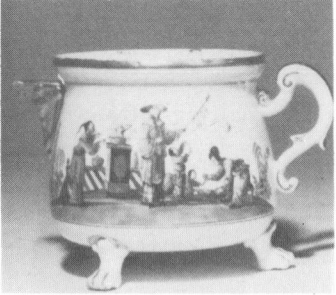

A Meissen Chinoiserie cream pot, with gilt foliage scroll spout and enriched handle, painted in the manner of J. G. Herold with Chinese figures, blue crossed swords mark and gilder's H., c. 1728, 16.5 cm. wide. **£1,200-£1,600**

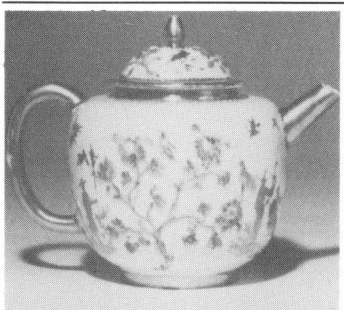

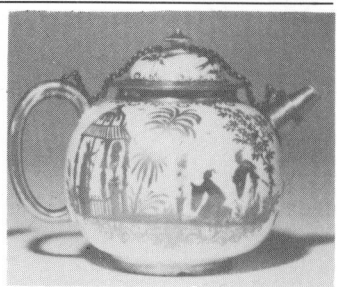

A Meissen globular teapot and cover, moulded with prunus and painted in puce, gilt at Augsburg in the Seuter workshop with Chinoiserie figures, minute chips to spout and finial, 1725-30, 17 cm. wide. **£2,500-£3,500**

A Meissen Hausmalerei gold Chinese globular teapot and domed cover, gilt at Augsburg by Bartolomaüs Seuter with Chinese in pagodas and on terraces, with silver gilt chain attachment, minor chips to foot rim, one chip to rim, interior of cover chipped, c. 1725, 16.5 cm. wide. **£2,500-3,500**

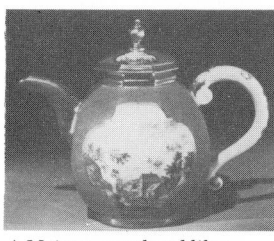

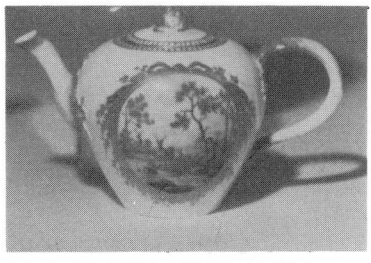

A Meissen powdered lilac octagonal oviform teapot and cover, the panels to the sides painted with a stag hunting scene and figures on a roadway to a harbour, within gilt surround and with gilt rims, spout and finial, the handle with indianische Blumen, blue crossed swords mark, each piece with gilder's mark 6, the base with Dreher's mark three circles, c. 1734. **£2,000-2,500**

A Meissen (Marcolini) baluster teapot and cover, handle restored, blue crossed swords and star marks, c. 1780, 19.5 cm. high. **£180-250**

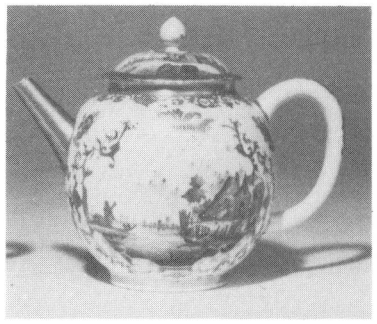

A Meissen teapot and cover, painted with European figures, within gilt and Böttger-lustre, iron-red, puce and gold Laub-und-Bandelwerk cartouches, flanked by sprays of indianische Blumen, cover restored, minor chips to spout, blue crossed swords mark, and gilder's number 39, c. 1730, 17 cm. wide. **£600-900**

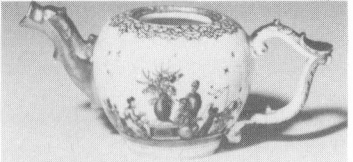

A Meissen Chinoiserie miniature teapot, with scroll handle and gilt spout, painted by C. F. Herold with Oriental families, beneath gilt Laub-und-Bandelwerk, blue crossed swords mark and gilder's number 45, c. 1730, 14.5 cm. wide. **£800-£1,200**

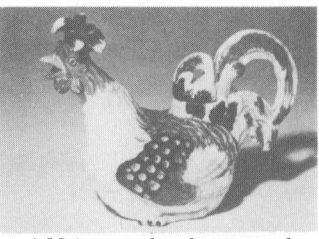

A Meissen cockerel teapot and cover, naturalistically modelled by J. J. Kändler, painted in colours in iron-red, black, green and puce, c. 1740, repair to beak and cover, 21 cm. wide. **£1,200-£1,500**

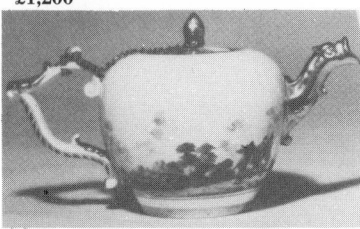

A Meissen globular teapot and a cover, painted by B. G. Haüer with mounted figures in a continuous river landscape, with bird's head spout enriched in puce, iron-red and gilt, the cover with chain attachment, finial repaired, blue crossed swords mark, gilder's mark a dot, c. 1740, 20 cm. wide. **£900-1,200**

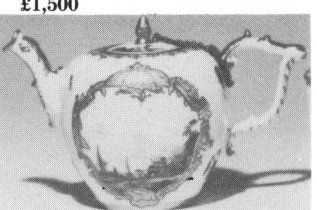

A Meissen dated teapot and cover, decorated with a courting couple before an obelisk bearing the date 1744 , blue crossed swords mark, the cover and base with gilder's mark 9, silver chain attachment, 18.5 cm. wide. **£5,000-7,000**
Dated or documentary pieces are extremely rare and it is quite easy to overlook the date, which is often incorporated in a architectural feature. Without the date, this piece could be expected to realise a fraction of this price — £1,500-2,500

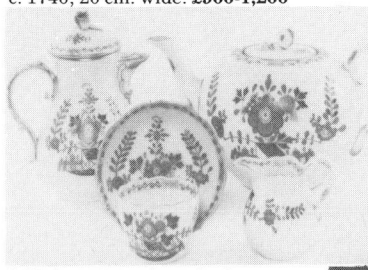

A Meissen tea set, each piece painted in polychrome enamels and gilding, in Oriental taste, crossed swords in underglaze-blue, painted numerals, 20th C. **£450-650**

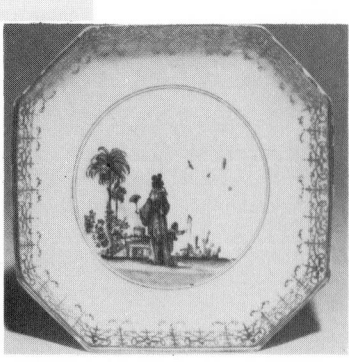

A Meissen Chinoiserie square teapot-stand, the central medallion with a Chinese lady holding a fan, with gilt scroll pattern border, blue crossed swords mark and gilder's mark H, c. 1730, 15 cm. wide. **£800-£1,000**

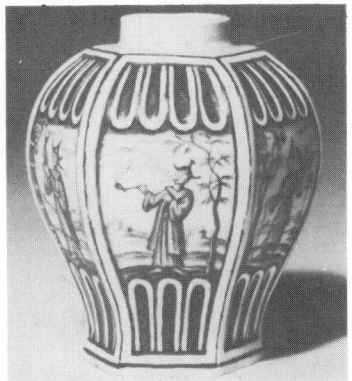

An early Meissen Hausmalerei hexagonal teacaddy, painted in the manner of Ignaz Preissler in Schwarzlot with Chinoiserie figures in landscapes, minor chip repair to foot rim, former's mark of Rehschuh, c. 1720, 9 cm. high. **£700-900**

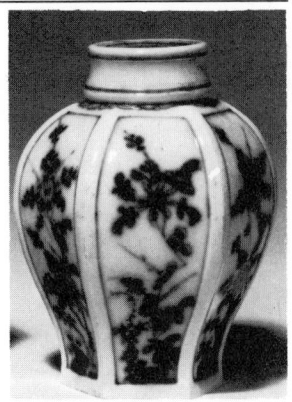

A Meissen blue and white octagonal teacaddy and cover, painted with flowering plants issuing from rockwork, 1725-30, 9.5 cm. high. **£300-450** *Underglaze-blue was never a successful method of decoration on early Meissen. This piece exhibits the characteristic smudgy effect.*

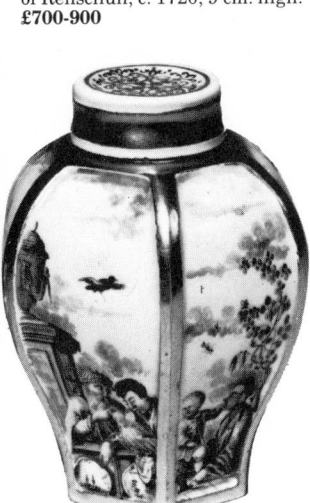

A Meissen Chinoiserie hexagonal teacaddy and cover, painted with six scenes, of a mother about to feed her baby beneath a hanging, a showman with a monkey on a barrel, a seated lady with pet birds, a mother putting on her child's shoe, a lady and an old man talking on a terrace beneath a vase and a bird catcher with a bird on a staff beneath a palm tree, the raised ribs gilt, blue, enamel crossed swords mark, c. 1725, 9.75 cm. high. **£10,000-£12,000**

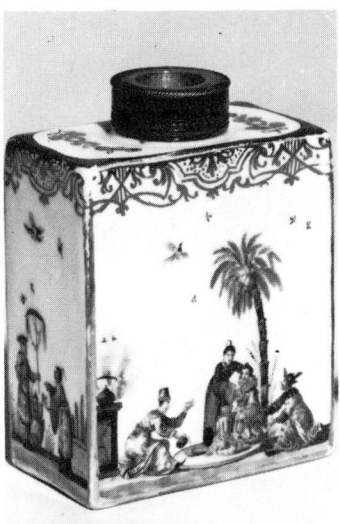

A Meissen Chinoiserie teacaddy, painted by C. F. Herold with numerous Chinamen, the upper border with gilt scrollwork, later silver mount to neck, blue crossed swords mark and impressed Dreher's mark probably for Seidel, and gilder's mark 44. **£900-1,200**

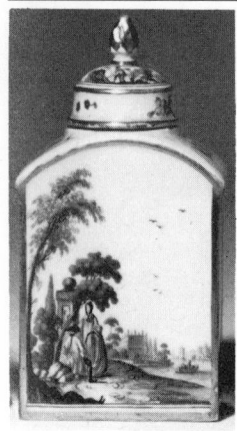

A Meissen teacaddy and cover, painted with figures in landscapes with tall trees, the shoulders with deutsche Blumen and the rims gilt, blue crossed swords mark and Pressnummer 34, c. 1740, 13 cm. high. **£1,200-£1,500**

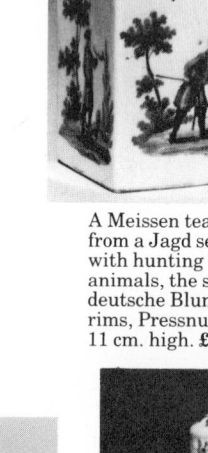

A Meissen teacaddy and a cover, from a Jagd service, painted with hunting figures and animals, the shoulder with deutsche Blumen and with gilt rims, Pressnummer 26, c. 1745, 11 cm. high. **£900-1,100**

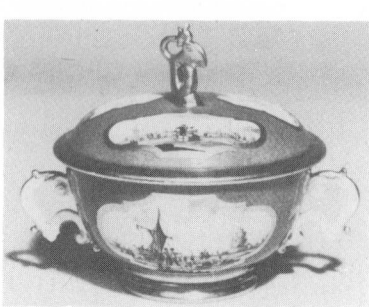

A Meissen powdered purple ground tureen and cover, painted with shaped quatrefoil panels of merchants, reserved in gilt panels, finial restored, blue crossed swords mark, c. 1740, 15 cm. diam. **£1,100-1,600**

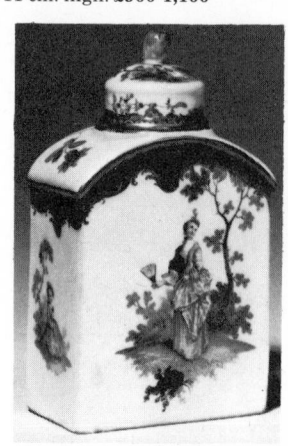

A Meissen teacaddy and cover, with blue scale borders, painted with figures in landscape vignettes, chip to bud finial, blue crossed swords and dot mark, c. 1765, 12 cm. high. **£500-750**

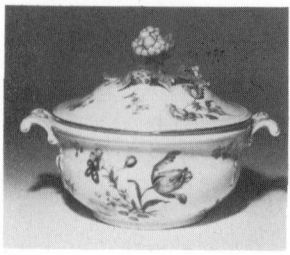

A Meissen circular two-handled tureen and cover, with Ozier border, painted with deutsche Blumen, blue crossed swords mark, Pressnummer 20, c. 1745, restored, 32 cm. wide. **£600-900**

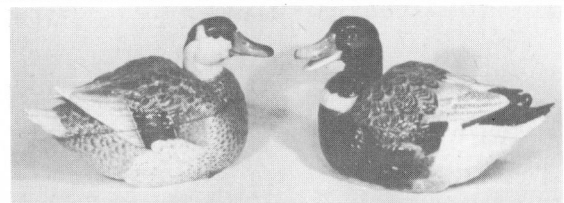

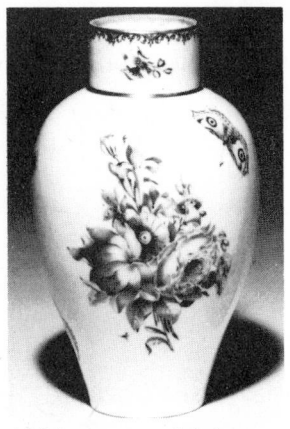

A pair of Meissen Marcolini duck tureens and covers, naturalistically modelled by Lück with brown, grey, puce and blue feather markings, their beaks in yellow and orange tones, blue crossed swords, star and 4 marks, c. 1780, 28.5 cm. long. **£3,000-4,000**

A Meissen vase, painted en camaieu rose with sprays of flowers and scattered butterflies and insects, the rim with gilt scrolling foliage, blue crossed swords mark, Pressnummer 21, c. 1760, 20.5 cm. high. **£400-600**

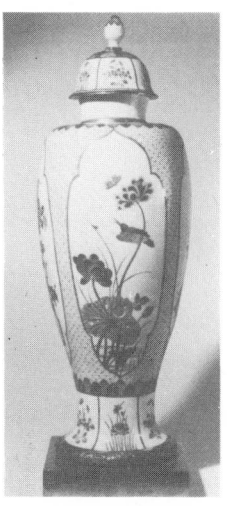

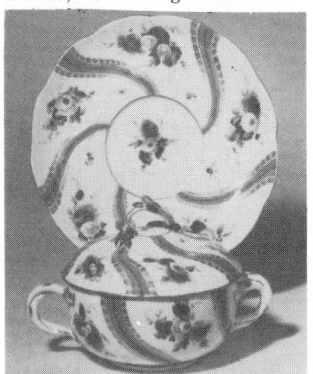

A Meissen tureen cover and stand, painted with spiral panels of puce flowers divided by green and gilt bands, blue crossed swords and dot mark, Pressnummer 34, c. 1765, the stand 22.5 cm. diam. **£750-950**
This piece is in Sèvres style, which had become prominent by this date.

A Meissen famille verte Augustus Rex vase and cover, the four panels painted with birds perched on water lilies and hibiscus within ogival green surround on iron-red cell pattern ground, within borders of manganese and ochre petals, with ormolu foot rim, the finial and the neck replacements, crack to lower part, a hole drilled in one side and another in the base, blue AR monogram mark, c. 1728, overall height 70 cm., height of the porcelain 64 cm. **£3,000-4,000**
This vase evidently once formed part of a garniture. A smaller vase, once perhaps associated with the present piece, is in the Ralph Wark Collection, Jacksonville, Florida.

MENNECY

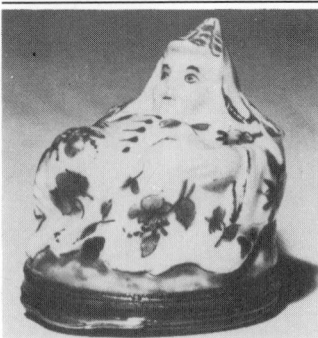

A Mennecy Chinoiserie snuff box, with silver mounts, painted with flowers, the contemporary mounts with bracket thumbpiece, the mounts with illegible décharge, c. 1745. **£700-1,000**

MENNECY

- factory founded in 1734
- in 1748 forbidden to copy Vincennes and moved to Mennecy
- milky white body with thick clear glaze
- early pieces can be slightly marred by black pitting
- most typical decoration is small flowers in the German style
- pieces virtually never gilded, because of royal patronage granting Vincennes and Sèvres sole right to gilding
- don't mistake the simplicity of Mennecy in comparison to Sèvres — for lack of quality, as this small factory produced some exquisite wares which now command high prices

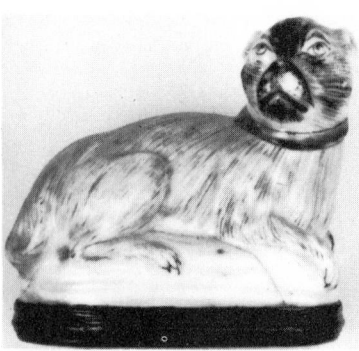

A Mennecy silver-mounted snuff box and cover, modelled as a recumbent pug dog with yellow and black fur marking and blue collar, cracked, the mounts with the décharge of Julien Berthe and Paris date letter for 1750, 7 cm. wide. **£300-400**

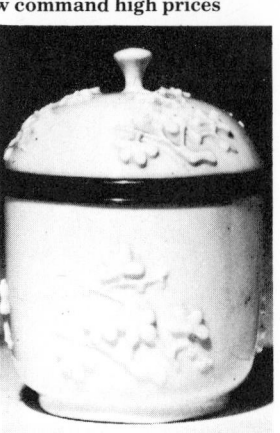

A pair of Mennecy white silver-mounted circular pots and covers, with reeded mounts, incised DV marks, the silver with the décharge of Julien Berthe, the porcelain, c. 1755, both covers cracked, 10 cm. high. **£180-250**. If perfect: **£300-400**

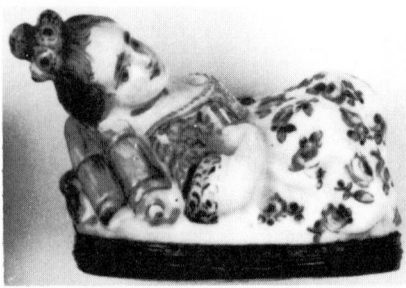

A Mennecy silver-mounted snuff box and cover, the cover painted with bouquets of flowers, the mounts with the décharge of Julien Berthe and Paris date letter for 1759, 8 cm. wide. **£1,200-1,600**

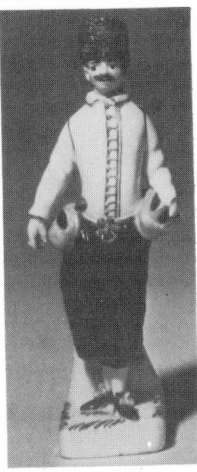

A Mennecy figure of a Turk, in black and red fur cap, yellow and gilt edged jacket and black apron, neck repaired, incised DV mark, c. 1750, 16 cm. high. **£400-£600**
The somewhat stiff modelling is typical of French soft paste porcelain. The difficulty in achieving figures with poise or movement was due to the innate properties of the porcelain, which tended to collapse in the kiln.

NAPLES

- factory founded in 1771
- porcelain has good translucency with a strong white paste
- strong neo-classical influence in the 1780's
- came under French ownership and influence in the early 19th C.
- mark was a crowned N although this was also used by other factories in the 19th C.
- factory closed in 1821
- 'Naples' is a term used to cover some late 19th C. porcelain which copied the style of this factory

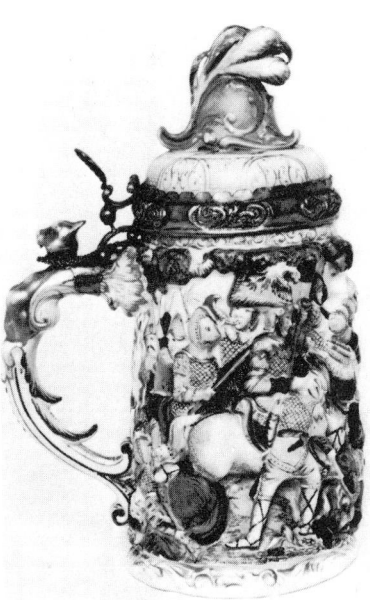

Two 'Naples' tankards, moulded and brightly coloured with a mediaeval battle scene, gilt bronze mounts, chips, 25.5 and 25.8 cm., marks in underglaze-blue, late 19th C. **£250-350**

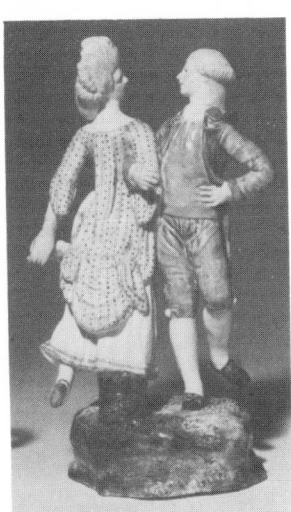

A Naples dancing group of a young man and woman, in green, puce, yellow and white, her left hand restored, c. 1780, 19.5 cm. high. **£1,000-1,200**

NAPLES-NYMPHENBERG

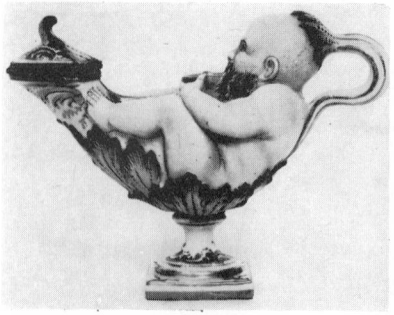

A 'Naples' inkwell and liner, of
Roman oil-lamp inspiration, as
Silenus holding a bowl to his lips
and reclining upon acanthus
leaves, hinged cover, gilt details,
10.5 cm., crowned N in
underglaze-blue, late 19th C.
£80-120

NYMPHENBURG

- **factory founded in the late
  1740's but the main production
  started in 1753**
- **J. J. Ringler was employed as
  arcanist**
- **from 1757 a fine milky white
  porcelain was produced**
- **the porcelain is of great quality
  and virtually flawless**
- **F. A. Bustelli modelled some
  excellent figures from 1754-63**
- **J. P. Melchior was chief
  modeller from 1797-1810**
- **the factory still exists**

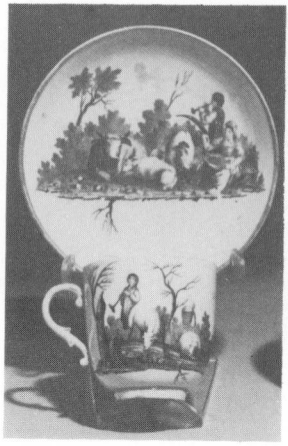

A Nymphenberg coffee cup and
saucer, painted with vignettes of
piping shepherds, shepherdesses,
sheep and cows, gilt rims,
impressed Bavarian shield
marks, c. 1765. **£800-1,200**

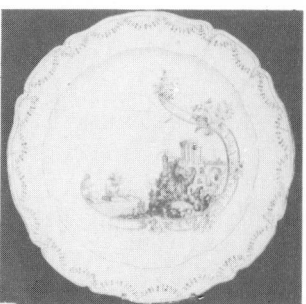

A large Nymphenberg shaped
circular dish, the centre painted
with a capriccio view of the
temple at Tivoli, enriched with
coloured flowers, the border with
swags in green and gold, blue
hexagram mark, 1763-67 and
impressed Bavarian shield,
between B and 3, 36 cm. diam.
£1,000-1,200
*Note on this transitional rococo/
neo-classical design, that the
centre is of a typical asymmetrical
form, while the border is
decorated in the restrained
manner of the later style.*

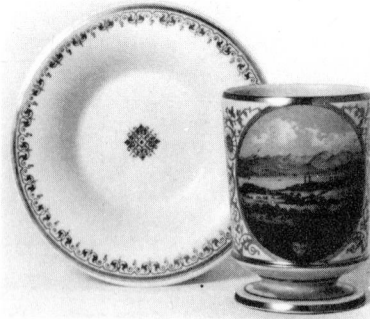

A Nymphenberg topographical
cabinet cup and saucer, the cup
painted with a view of Lindau
within a gilt scroll border, the
saucer with a gilt border at the
rim, saucer 13.4 cm., impressed
shield mark, mid to late 19th C.
£250-350

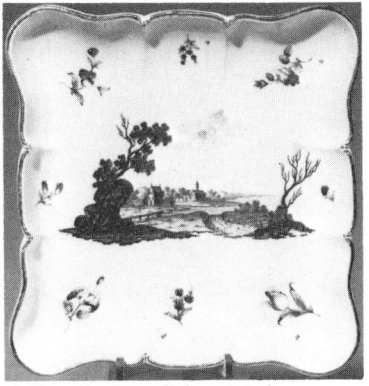

A Nymphenberg dish, painted
with a river landscape vignette
with buildings, with a gilt rim,
impressed Bavarian shield mark
and incised 43 XH, c. 1760,
25 cm. wide. **£400-600**

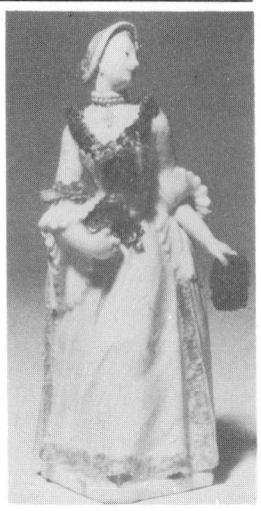

A Nymphenberg figure of a
young woman, modelled by
Franz Anton Bustelli, in pink,
yellow and blue, on shaped
triangular base, neck and left
arm repaired, c. 1758, 16 cm.
high. **£1,200-1,500**
*The flat angular base suggests a
very early date, c. 1754, when
young Bustelli joined
Nymphenberg and was still
under the influence of J. P. R.
Haertl, another modeller. The
slightly stiff appearance also
suggests an early date before
Bustelli developed his own
inimitable style.*

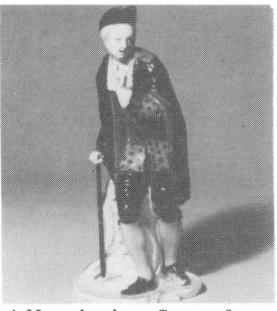

A Nymphenberg figure of
Anselmo or L'Abbe from the
Commedia dell'Arte, modelled
by Franz Anton Bustelli, in
black and grey cloak, waistcoat
and breeches, restorations to his
cane and part of the base and
hat, c. 1760, 20 cm. high. **£5,500-
£7,500**
*Franz Anton Bustelli perhaps
modelled the most elegant figures
in 18th C. German porcelain.*

A Nymphenberg figure of a
Chinese archer, modelled by
Franz Anton Bustelli, in pink,
grey, iron-red, gilt, puce and
yellow robe, on shaped semi-
circular base, his left arm
restored, the clasp to his belt
impressed with a Bavarian
shield mark, the back of the base
incised 'I.D.', c. 1765, 21.5 cm.
high. **£2,500-3,500**
*The use of the factory mark as a
decorative feature on the figure is
a particularly enchanting
Bavarian rococo touch.*

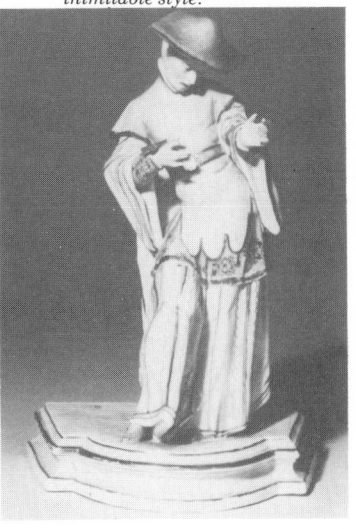

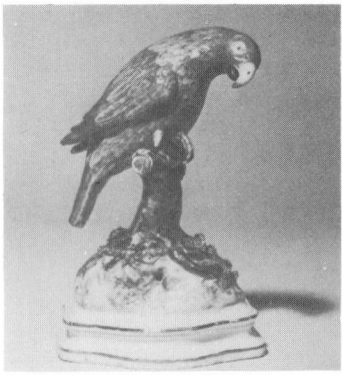

A Nymphenberg figure of a parrot, modelled by Dominicus Auliczek, in green, yellow, red, blue and gilt, chips, impressed Bavarian shield mark and I D, 15.5 cm. high, c. 1765. **£1,800-£2,100**

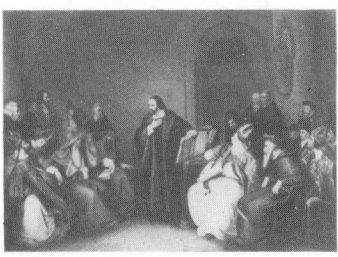

A Nymphenberg rectangular plaque, painted by Fredrich Auguste Schmidt with the Trial of Galileo, signed, impressed mark, in a carved giltwood frame, 25 by 36 cm. **£1,400-1,600**

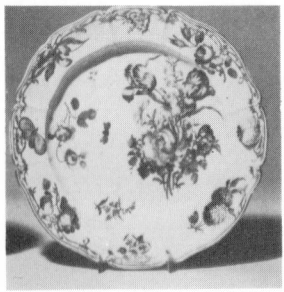

A Nymphenberg plate, painted with sprays of flowers and insects within the blue and gilt shaped rim, minute rim chips, impressed 2, c. 1765, 25.5 cm. diam. **£700-900**

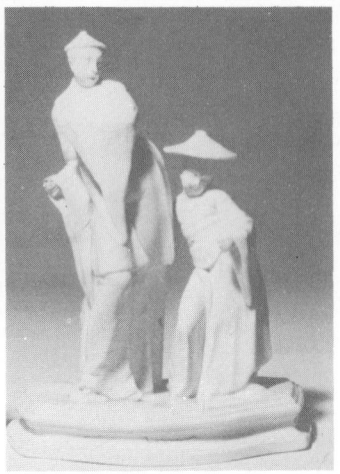

A Nymphenberg white Chinoiserie group, models modified from Franz Anton Bustelli, hands of both figures chipped, impressed Bavarian shield mark and incised S (inversed) and DI, c. 1765. **£1,400-1,600**
One of several Bustelli creations reworked by the Bossierer Peter Anton Seefried, shortly after Bustelli's death.

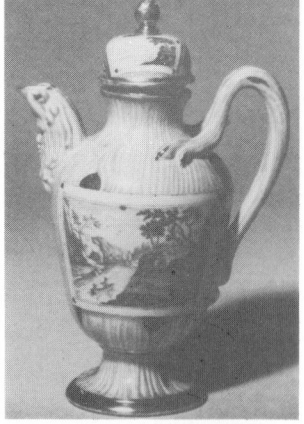

A Nymphenberg 'Bois Simulé' jug and domed cover, the short spout moulded with a bearded and horned mask, reserved with panels painted en camaieu rose with figures in boats and in river landscapes, impressed Bavarian shield mark, c. 1780, 16.5 cm. high. **£400-600**

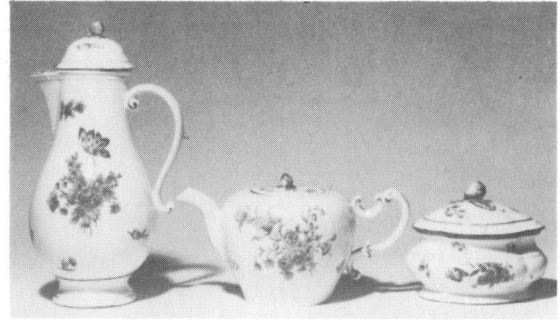

A Nymphenberg part tea and coffee service, painted in green, black and iron-red, comprising: coffee pot, teapot and cover, sugar box and cover, and eight teacups and saucers, coffee pot with minute chip to spout, teapot with chips to spout and cover recess, sugar box cracked and one cup chipped, impressed Bavarian shield marks, c. 1765. **£1,000-1,500**

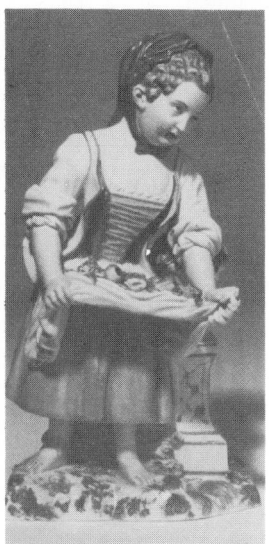

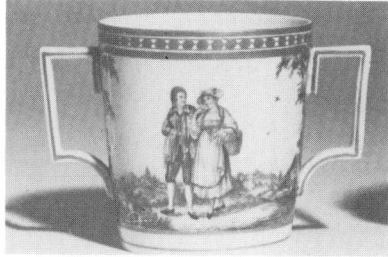

A Nyon cup and later cover and stand, the cup painted with wayfarers resting on a path and a young man and woman walking, beneath gilt rim, the cover and stand painted with grapes, the cover repaired, the cup with blue fish mark, c. 1790. **£250-350**

An Ottweiler figure of a girl, in bright colours, the much fire-cracked base repaired, probably in the factory, c. 1770, 23 cm. high. **£1,800-2,300**

NYON

- **factory founded in the early 1780's**
- **good hard paste body**
- **after Zürich the best Swiss factory**
- **factory closed in 1860**

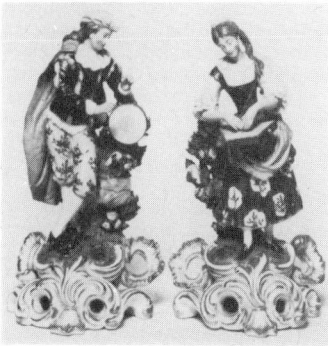

A pair of Paris 'Derby' figures on gilt scroll base, 20 cm., crossed arrows in underglaze-blue, late 19th C. **£210-230**

PARIS

SAMSON, EDME ET CIE (PARIS)

- factory opened in Paris in 1845
- reproduced wares of virtually every other factory (both Continental and Oriental)
- their fakes of Meissen and Chinese porcelain are excellent
- their English soft-paste porcelain fakes are easier to detect, as they used a Continental hard-paste body
- Samson claims that all wares have an 'S' contained within the mark — however this can be easily removed by the unscrupulous
- more pieces are attributed to Samson than they could possibly have made

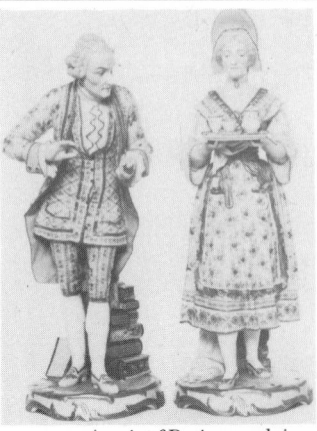

A pair of Paris porcelain figures of a maid bringing a tray of chocolate and a gentleman standing before a pile of books, tray chipped, minor damage, 37.5 and 41.2 cm., printed green anchor marks, late 19th C. **£250-350**

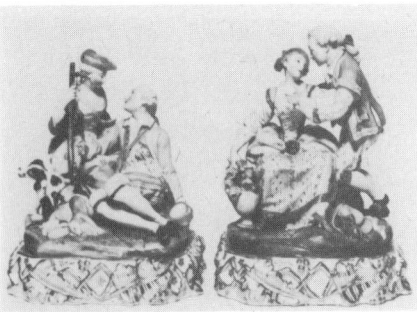

A pair of Paris biscuit porcelain groups, coloured and gilt, 24 cm., c. 1870. **£350-400**

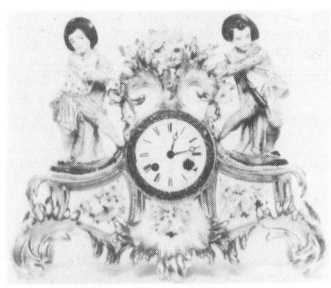

A Paris clock case, surmounted by two young boys dressed as a fisherman or a hunter, with gilt foliate scrolls and painted with panels of pink roses, minor chips, length 37 cm., the dial and movement signed 'Valery, Paris', mid 19th C. **£300-400**

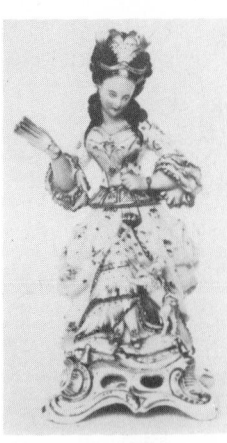

A rare and amusing Paris veilleuse, modelled as an eighteenth century belle, her torso detaching at the bodice to form a teapot filled through a removable chignon and issuing through her right arm, the bordeloue-shaped burner inserting from the rear beneath the seat, minor chips, 35 cm., c. 1840. **£200-300**

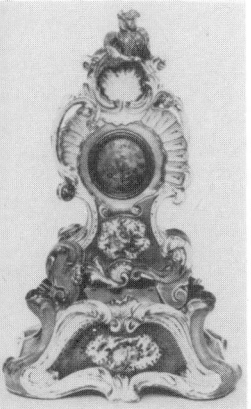

A Paris clock case and stand, the rococo scrolled case painted with panels of summer flowers and birds on green, pink and blue grounds, gilt details, some damage and restoration, 55 cm., MA in underglaze-blue, mid 19th C. **£250-400**

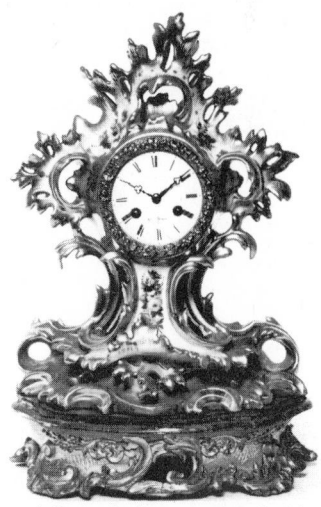

A Paris clock case, painted with flower sprays and puce details on an apple green ground, enamelled dial, 30.5 cm., on giltwood stand, mid 19th C. **£150-200**

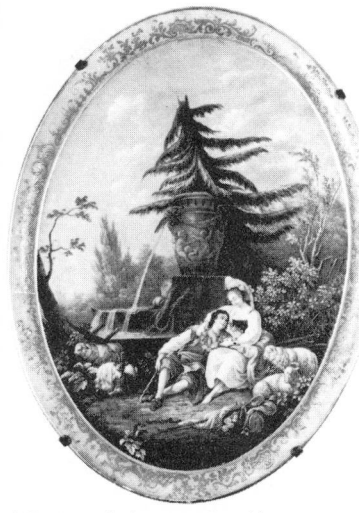

A Paris oval plaque, painted by Binet, signed, within a raised rim with gilt scrolls on a pale blue border, 44.8 cm., mid to late 19th C. **£400-550**

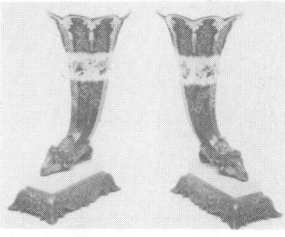

A pair of Paris cornucopia vases, with beaded ornament in gold and gilt on a maroon ground, the white centres painted in colours, on white marble bases with ormolu borders, 12½ in., mid 19th C. **£320-400**

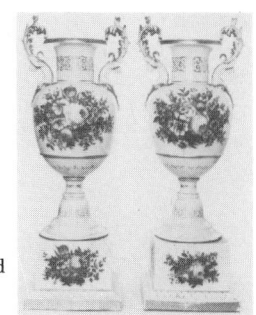

A pair of large Paris vases and stands, 82.5 cm., late 19th C. **£680-750**

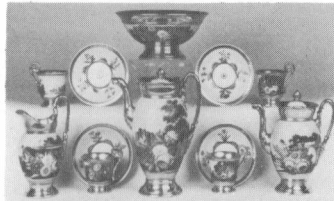

A Paris porcelain tea service, in the Empire style, comprising: a teapot and cover, a hot water jug and cover, a milk jug, a sugar bowl, a slop bowl and eight cups and saucers, restored. **£1,450-£1,650**

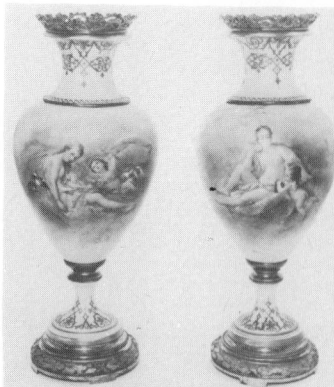

A pair of Paris vases, 33.8 cm., c. 1850. **£235-265**

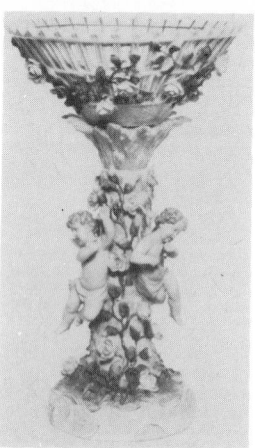

A Plaue centrepiece, the detachable circular bowl pierced and applied with trails of roses, the stem encircled by three putti, chips, 40.8 cm., crossed parallel lines in underglaze-blue, c. 1900. **£150-250**

A pair of gilt metal mounted Paris vases, each painted by P. Soustre, signed, mounted with a pierced rim and circular laurel wreath foot, 63.5 cm., c. 1880. **£500-800**

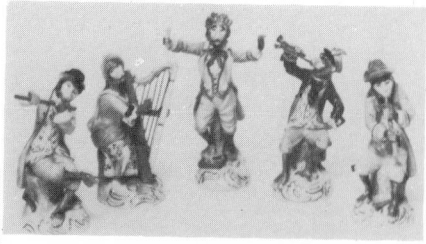

A Potschappel 12-piece monkey band, of Meissen inspiration, initials mark in underglaze-blue, 13 to 16.5 cm., late 19th C. **£400-£500**

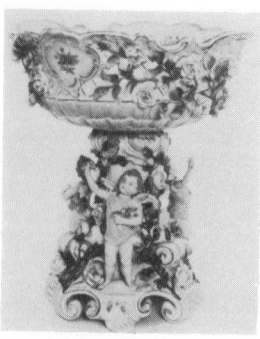

A Plaue centrepiece, painted with floral sprays and applied with floral trails and three putti, chips, 35 cm., crossed parallel lines in underglaze-blue, c. 1900. **£200-300**

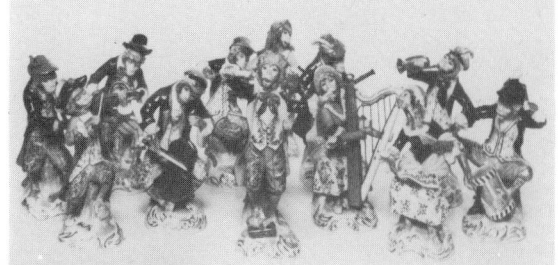

A Potschappel monkey band, of Meissen inspiration, 14 to 16.5 cm., monogram and Dresden mark in underglaze-blue, c. 1900. **£350-400**

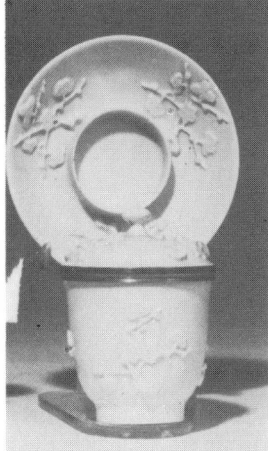

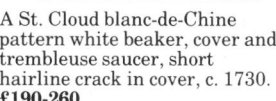

A St. Cloud blanc-de-Chine pattern white beaker, cover and trembleuse saucer, short hairline crack in cover, c. 1730. **£190-260**
St. Cloud relied heavily on blanc-de-Chine porcelain designs applied to European forms.

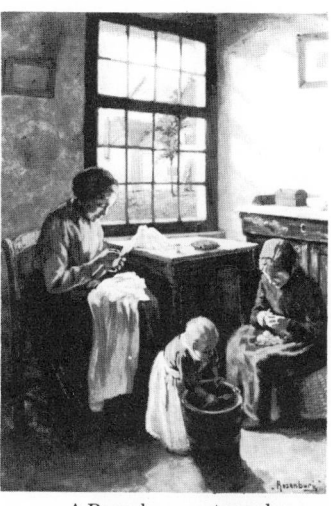

A Rozenburg rectangular porcelain plaque, painted by Albert Neuhaus, signed and with printed marks, gilt and ebonised wood frame, 33 by 25.5 cm. **£700-900**

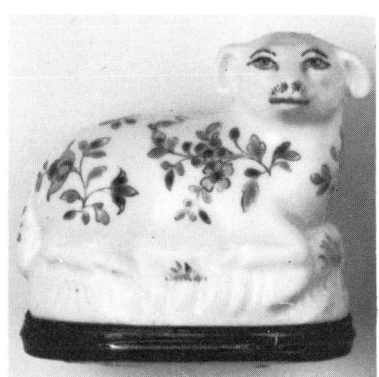

A St. Cloud silver-mounted snuff box and cover, modelled as a recumbent sheep, painted with sprays of flowers in the Kakiemon palette, the mounts with décharge of Julien Berthe, 1750-56, 7 cm. wide. **£900-1,200**

ST. CLOUD

- **factory produced wares from late 17th C. to the 1770's**
- **early pieces heavily potted**
- **glaze thick and clear, frequently showing pitting**
- **body has creamy or ivory tone**
- **until mid 1730's pieces mainly decorated in underglaze-blue**
- **also specialised in pieces influenced by the blanc-de-Chine wares**
- **after mid 1730's polychrome wares produced**

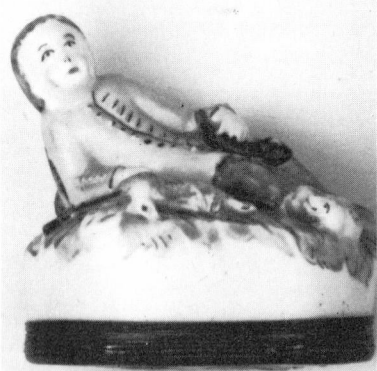

A pair of St. Cloud white artichoke-moulded coffee cups and trembleuse saucers, c. 1730. **£280-350**
This is a very typical form of St. Cloud.

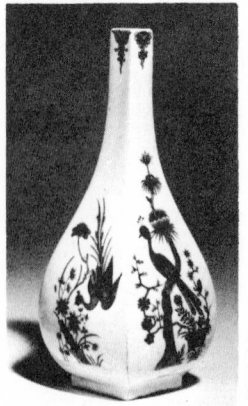

A St. Cloud silver-mounted snuff box and cover, modelled as a recumbent sportswoman, in yellow and blue, the cover moulded with coloured flowers, the silver mounts with décharge of Julien Berthe and the date letter possibly for 1754, 8 cm. wide. **£700-900**

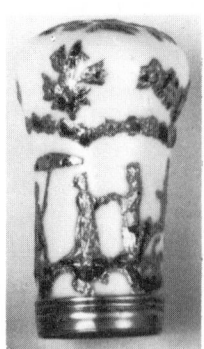

A St. Cloud cane-handle, decorated in the Berlin style with figures in gold and coloured enamels, gilt metal mount, .c. 1725, 6 cm. high. **£350-500**

A Samson sake bottle, painted in the Kakiemon palette in the Meissen style, the rim with formal foliage, 21.5 cm. high. **£200-250**

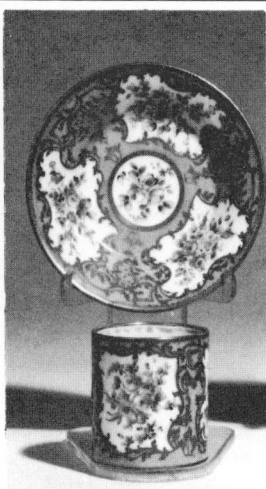

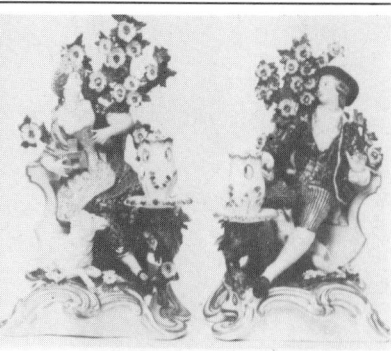

A pair of Samson 'Derby' candlesticks, each modelled as an eighteenth century shepherd or shepherdess wearing colourful rustic clothes, chips, 26 cm., painted crown mark erased, late 19th C. £250-350

A Samson pink ground 'Sèvres' coffee can and saucer, painted in colours with bouquets of flowers outlined in gilt, with gilt dentil rims, minor chip to saucer. £40-80

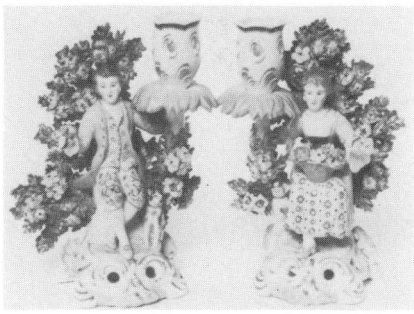

A pair of Samson 'Chelsea' bocage candlestick groups, 16 and 16.5 cm., gilt anchor, late 19th C. £120-180

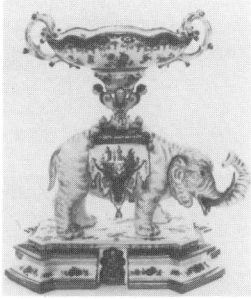

A Samson 'Meissen' comport and stand, modelled after Kändler, picked out with Chinoiseries in the manner of Herold, the stand inset with Orientals, all scattered with indianische Blumen between gilt and iron-red borders, minor restoration, 35.5 cm., various pseudo-Meissen marks, c. 1880. £200-300

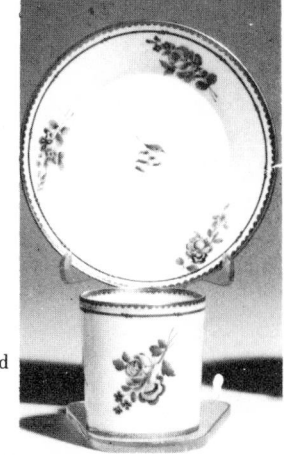

A Samson 'Sèvres' coffee can and saucer, painted in colours with flower sprays within blue line and gilt dash borders, with gilt dentil rims. £30-60

89

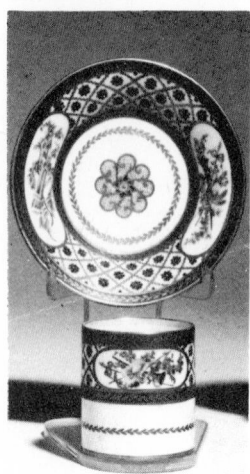

A Samson 'Sèvres' coffee can and saucer, painted in colours with amatory and musical trophies tied with ribbons among flowering plants divided by gilt trellis, between bands of gilt foliage. **£70-100**

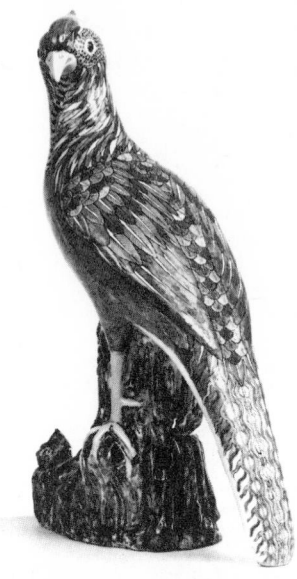

A Samson famille rose model of a pheasant, after a Chinese original, painted in iron-red, turquoise, blue, puce and yellow, the enamels chipped, with some repainting, 38 cm. high. **£200-£300**

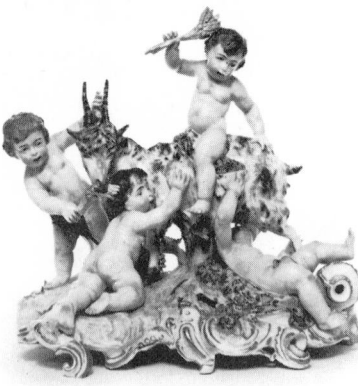

A Samson group of putti celebrating the harvest, the whole brightly coloured, minor damage, 36 cm., crossed swords in underglaze-blue, late 19th C. **£150-250**

A Samson 'Chelsea' group, modelled as Diana bathing in a stream and accompanied by three hand-maidens, the whole in pastel colours, minor restoration, gilt anchor, 38 cm., c. 1880. **£250-400**

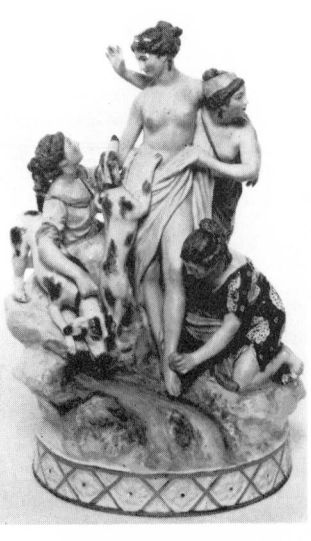

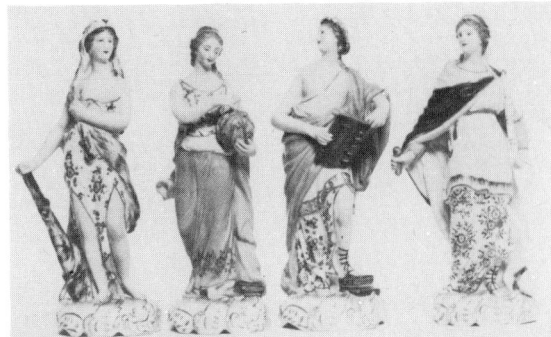

A set of four Samson figures, each modelled as an allegorical classical maiden, some restoration, 19.5 to 20.2 cm., crossed in underglaze-blue, late 19th C. **£150-300**

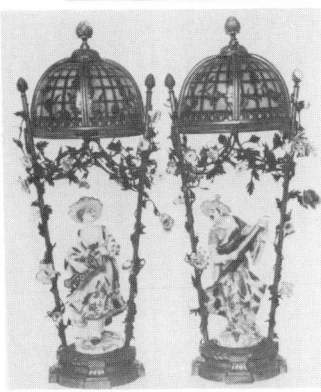

A pair of Samson 'Meissen' Malabar figures, within ormolu cupolas with stained glass flower trellis domes, the posts wreathed with ormolu and porcelain foliage and flowers, 17.5 cm., underglaze-blue crossed lines, late 19th C., pierced for electricity. **£300-450**

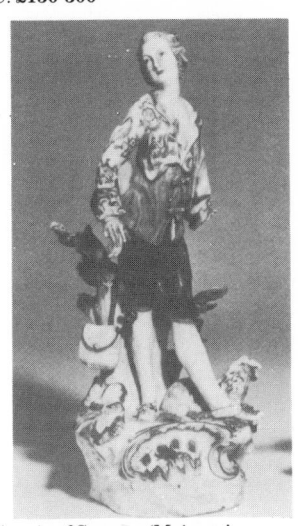

A pair of Samson 'Meissen' figures of a shepherd and a shepherdess, in brightly coloured clothes with recumbent sheep at their feet, chips, his left hand missing, minor repairs, blue crossed lines marks at back, both about 25.5 cm. high. **£150-250**

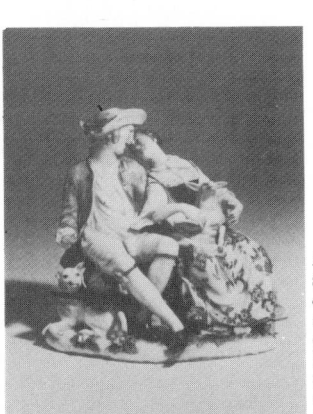

A Samson 'Meissen' group of shepherd lovers, after a model by J. J. Kändler, he in yellow hat and turquoise jacket, his companion with flowered skirt, his right hand and her feet missing, minor chips, blue crossed lines marks at back, 15 cm. high. **£350-450**

SAMSON

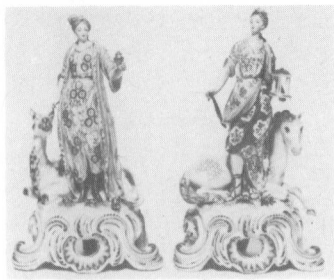

A pair of Samson figures of Continents, after Derby originals, 26 and 27 cm., crowned gilt BB monogram, late 19th C. **£170-200**

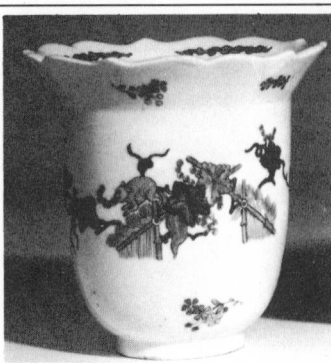

A Samson 'Chantilly' jardinière, painted in the Kakiemon palette, with the 'Squirrel' pattern, iron-red interlaced S mark, 14 cm. high. **£80-120**

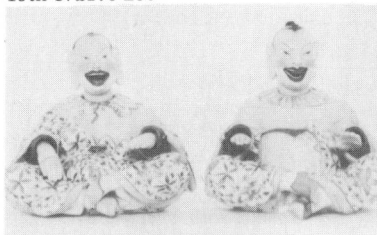

A pair of Samson nodding mandarins, in Meissen taste, each with counter-balanced head, tongue and hands, one hand and cuff damaged, 24 and 26 cm., crossed swords and S in underglaze-blue, late 19th C. **£300-500**

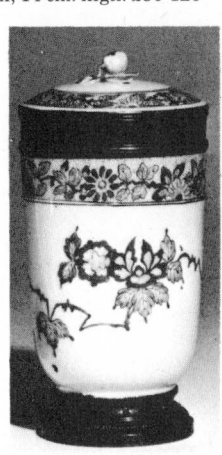

A Samson silver-mounted jar and cover, in the Chantilly style, painted in the Kakiemon palette on a seeded ground, firing crack to cover, iron-red hunting horn and interlaced S mark, 18 cm. high. **£70-100**

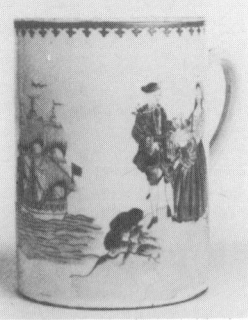

A Samson famille rose mug, painted with 'The Sailor's Farewell', iron-red 'made in France' mark, 18 cm. high. **£300-£400**

A Samson 'Sèvres' yellow ground monteith, painted with a parrot among flowering plants, the foliage handles enriched with gilding and with gilt rim, 30.5 cm. wide. **£80-140**

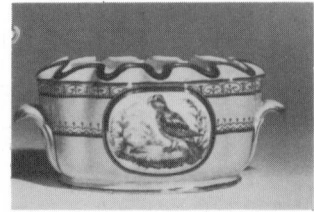

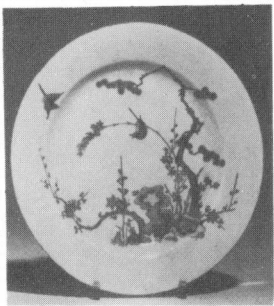

A Samson 'Meissen' plate, painted in the Kakiemon palette, enriched in gilding, with a chocolate rim, 24 cm. diam. **£150-200**

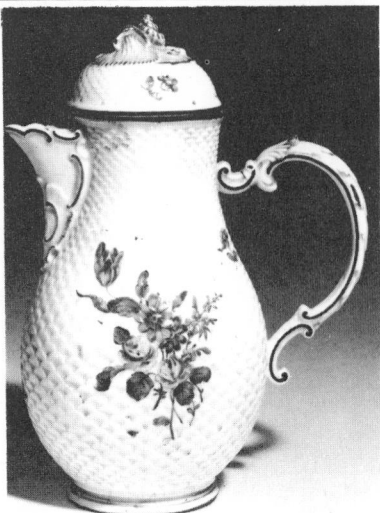

A Samson coffee pot and cover, in the Ludwigsburg style, the scale-moulded body painted in colours with flower sprays, firing crack to handle, 21 cm. high. **£100-150**

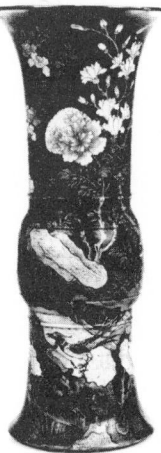

A Samson famille noire gu-shaped beaker vase, after Chinese originals, aubergine ES monogram mark, 47 cm. high. **£250-£350**

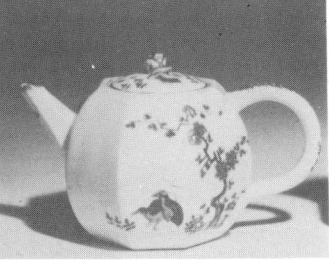

A Samson teapot and cover, in the Meissen style, painted in the Kakiemon palette with the grouse-pattern, inscribed in iron-red 'Poncif 1368' and interlaced S mark, 18 cm. wide. **£100-150**

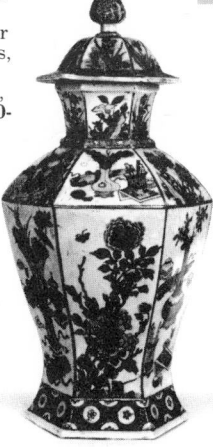

Left
A Samson famille verte jar and cover, after Chinese originals, painted on the body with chrysanthemum, peony and daisy alternating with vessels and precious emblems, firing crack with associated chip, finial cracked, iron-red ES monogram mark, 56 cm. high. **£300-400**

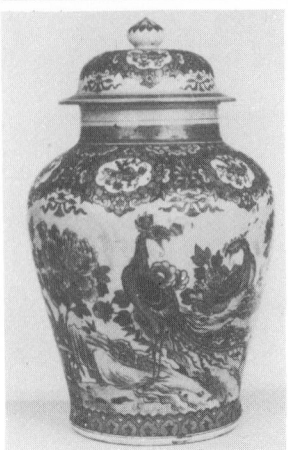

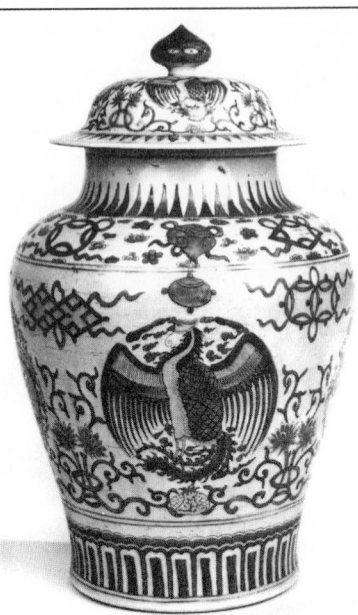

A Samson famille rose vase and cover, after Chinese originals, painted with a pair of pheasants perched on pierced rockwork beside peony on a garden terrace, the base with an extended firing crack, 49 cm. high. **£300-400**
A 19th C. Chinese example of this size would certainly be double the price, even if less well painted.

A Samson 'Wucai' vase and cover, painted with phoenix and dragon roundels divided by precious emblems and scrolling lotus, below bands of crustacea, emblems and stiff leaves at the neck, 42 cm. high. **£200-300**

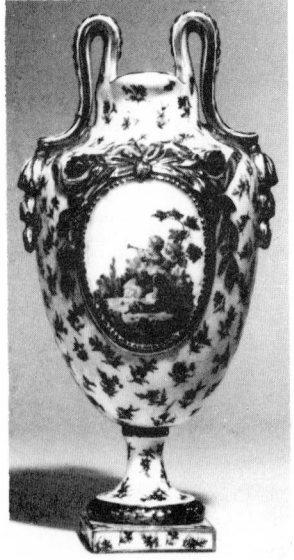

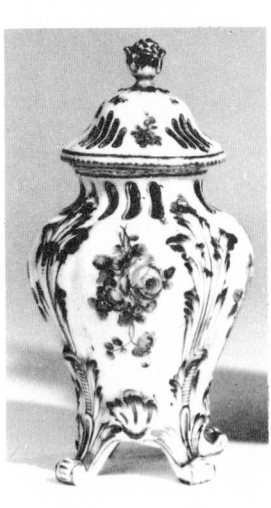

A Samson 'Sèvres' vase, painted in colours with a boy blowing a trumpet, within a moulded gilt cartouche, on a ground of scattered cornflowers, 33 cm. high. **£60-120**

A Samson pot pourri vase and cover, painted in colours with bouquets of flowers, enriched and gilt, 20 cm. high. **£50-80**

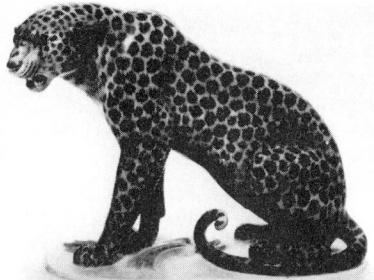

A Schwarzburger Werkstätten Für Porzellankunst model of a cheetah, the base with moulded modeller's monogram A.St., impressed running fox mark and shape number U1221, 40 cm., early 20th C. **£180-250**

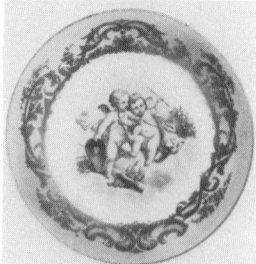

An outside decorated pink ground Sèvres bowl, painted with cherubs, gilding rubbed, 28.7 cm., cancelled printed mark, date code for 1847, the decoration later. **£150-250**

SÈVRES

- factory moved to Sèvres in 1756 from Vincennes where production started, c. 1740
- in early days copied Meissen and influenced by Kakiemon
- in 1750's factory began producing vases in large quantities
- most sought after ground colour is the yellow (jaune jonquille)
- plaques for furniture became popular in 1760's
- factory also noted for clock-cases, small sets for tea, coffee and chocolate, and boxes
- managed to discover the secret of hard-paste porcelain in 1770
- 'Jewelled porcelain' was introduced in 1773, used a technique of fusing enamels over gilt or silver foil

Not only was the Sèvres mark the second most copied mark after Meissen but also the style was emulated by numerous Paris factories. When a piece is described as 'Sèvres' it is almost certainly by one of these other factories.

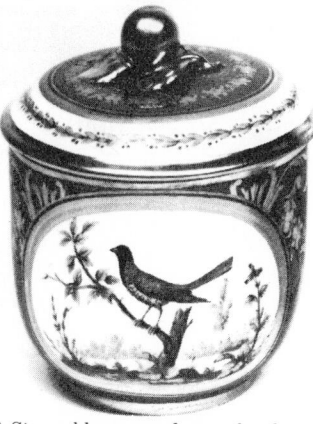

A Sèvres blue ground sugar bowl and cover, painted in colours with named birds, the base inscribed 'Bouvreuil, de l'isle Bourbon' and 'Bouvreuil, du Cap de Bonne Espérance', blue interlaced L marks enclosing the date letter for 1789, painter's mark of Evans, 11.5 cm. high. **£500-600**

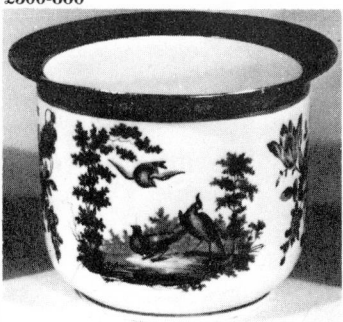

A Sèvres cache-pot, painted in colours with exotic birds on branches and in flight divided by bouquets of flowers, the upper side with gilt oeil de perdrix on the blue ground, with gilt dentil rim, blue interlaced L mark, c. 1800, 22 cm. diam. **£400-600**

95

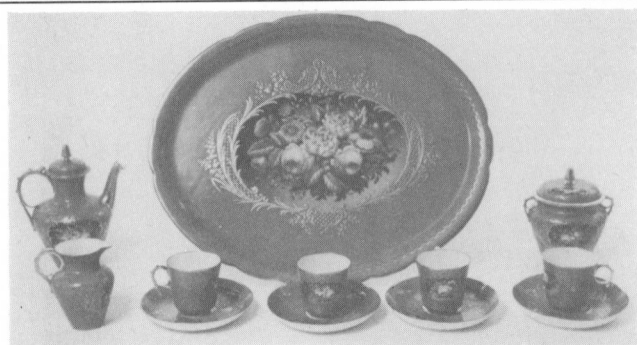

An outside decorated Sèvres chocolate set, 12 pieces, minor damage, tray: 45 cm., various printed and painted marks, some cancelled, incised Le 31-5, date codes for 1840 and 1842. **£650-£800**

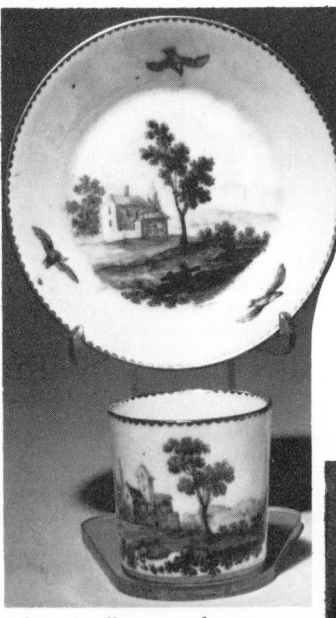

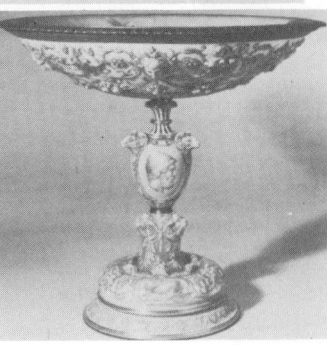

A Sèvres blue and white metal mounted centre dish, the bowl decorated with a scene from Classical mythology, the underside moulded and enriched in gilding with dragons and female masks suspending fruiting swags, the central oviform section to the stem with three profile portraits, the base painted with three oval panels of sea animals, date marks for 1851, 39.5 cm. diam. **£800-1,000**

A Sèvres coffee cup and saucer, painted in colours with buildings in landscapes and with exotic birds, the rims gilt, the saucer incised FDC, c. 1760. **£100-150**

A pair of Sèvres apple green ground coffee cups and saucers, painted with rose sprays, reserved within gilt surrounds, blue interlaced L marks enclosing the date letter for 1768. **£500-700**

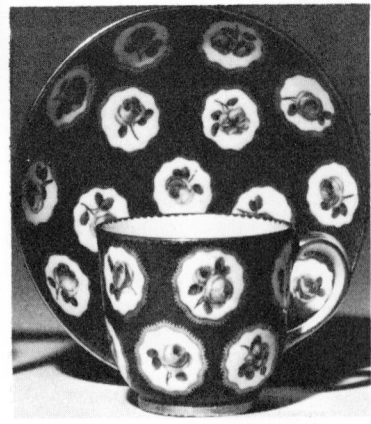

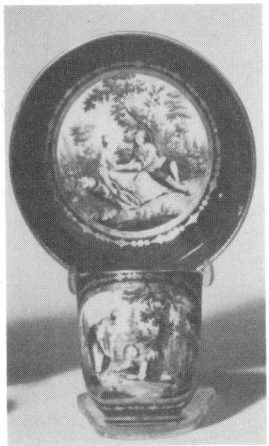

A Sèvres bleu nouveau cup and saucer, painted with lovers, the cup cracked, c. 1770. **£150-210**

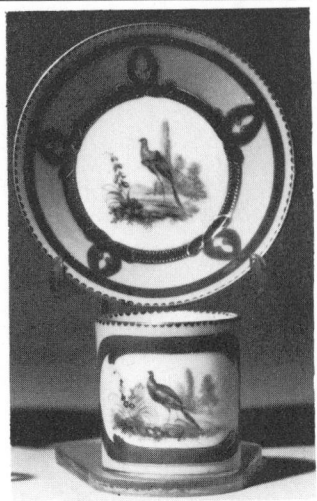

A Sèvres yellow ground coffee can and saucer, reserved with exotic birds in landscapes within apple green and gilt edged scroll cartouches, blue interlaced L marks, c. 1775. **£400-600**

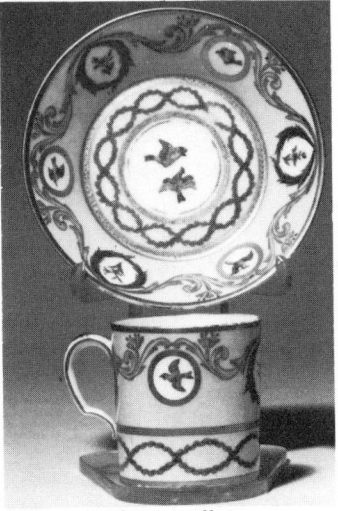

A Sèvres hard paste yellow ground coffee can and saucer, blue interlaced crowned L marks enclosing the date letter for 1780, painter's mark. **£300-400**

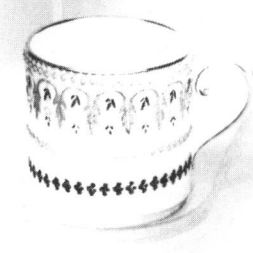

A Sèvres jewelled small coffee cup and saucer, decorated in pale blue, green, red and pink enamel enriched in gilding, gilt interlaced L marks, gilder's mark of Vincent, c. 1780. **£300-£400**

A Sèvres dessert service, 22 pieces, some with blue interlaced L marks enclosing the date letter for 1770 and various painter's marks, damaged: **£880-£1,100**. If perfect: **£1,500-£2,500**

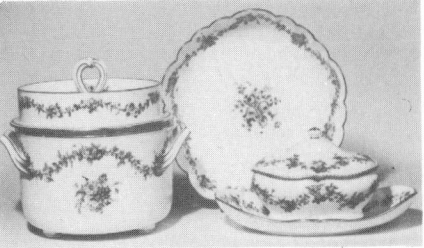

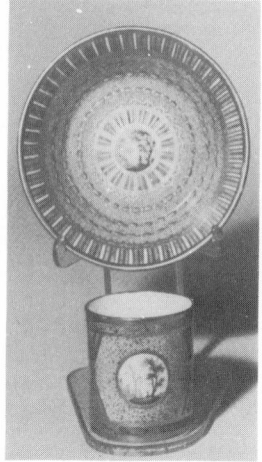

A Sèvres small coffee cup and saucer, small chip, blue interlaced L marks, double F's for 1783 and unidentified painter's mark. **£300-400**

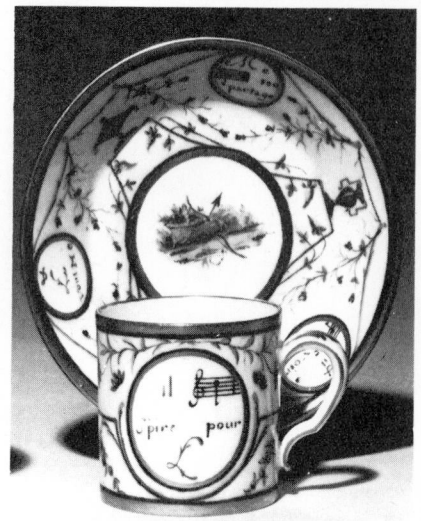

A Sèvres cylindrical coffee cup and saucer, painted in colours with a quiver of arrows beside a basket of flowers, reserved with roundels enclosing sentimental acrostics, blue interlaced L marks enclosing the date letter for 1788, painter's mark V, gilder's mark FM. **£400-600**

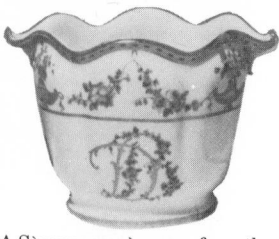

A Sèvres seau à verre, from the Du Barry service, painted with gilt D and floral B monograms, the border with gilt rings and blue vases suspending garlands of flowers, fire crack in base, chip to rim, blue interlaced L mark enclosing the date letter S for 1771 and painter's mark of Le Bel jeune, 16.5 cm. wide. **£350-£450**

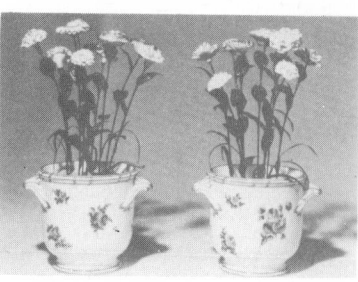

A pair of Sèvres seaux à bouteilles, enriched in gilt, filled with later green 'tôle peinte' stemmed flowers with Sèvres flowerheads, minor chips and repairs to the flowers, one seau with hair crack in base, blue interlaced L marks, c. 1765, overall height 32 cm. **£800-1,200**

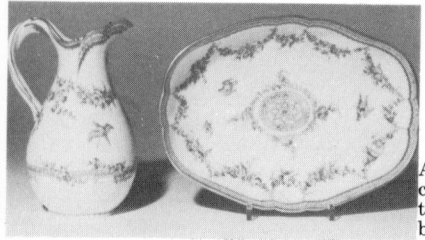

A Sèvres ewer and basin, blue crowned interlaced L marks and the date letter q for 1769, the basin 26 cm. wide. **£660-800**

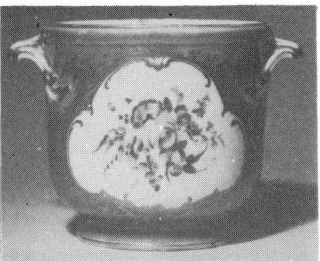

A Sèvres turquoise green jardinière, painted in colours with fruit and flower sprays within gilt ciselé C scroll and flowering foliage şurrounds with gilt rim, blue interlaced L mark, incise CL, painter's mark, c. 1770, minor rim chip, 24 cm. wide. **£550-750**

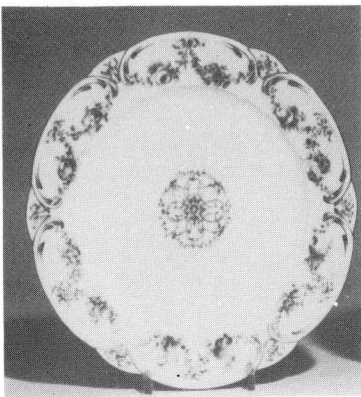

A Sèvres plate, from a service of Louis XV decorated en camaieu rose and gold, puce interlaced Ls enclosing the date letter D for 1756 and painter's mark of Noel, 24 cm. diam. **£700-900**

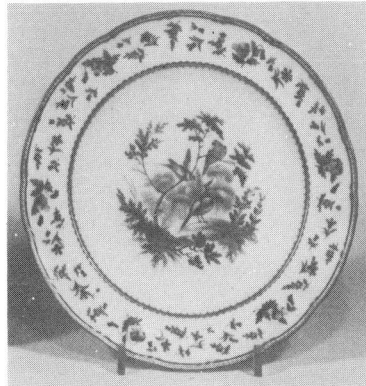

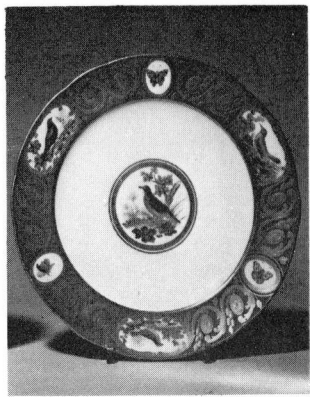

A Sèvres plate, painted with named birds, the turquoise green border reserved with three panels enclosing further birds alternating with roundels enclosing butterflies, enriched with gilt foliage scrolls with gilt rim, c. 1780, 24 cm. diam. **£300-£400**

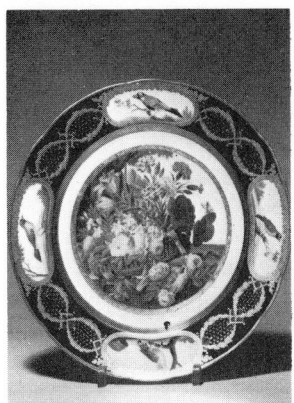

A Sèvres plate, painted in colours with a basket of flowers within a border of named birds, within gilt surrounds reserved on the blue ground, with gilt dentil rims, blue interlaced L mark, c. 1780, 23.5 cm. diam. **£400-500**

A pair of Sèvres plates, painted with colours with birds, the borders with cornflowers and pansies, with gilt dentil rims, blue interlaced L marks, date letter for 1792, painter's mark RB, one with minute rim chip, 24 cm. diam. **£400-600**

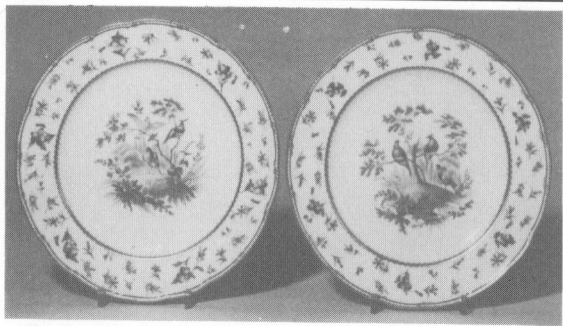

A pair of Sèvres plates, with gilt dash and dentil rims, blue interlaced L marks enclosing the date letter for 1792, 24 cm. diam. **£400-600**

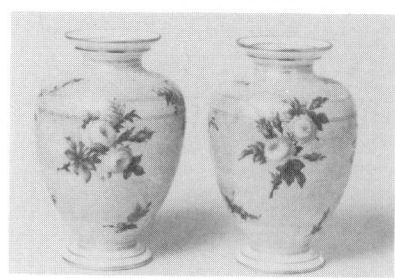

A pair of Sèvres vases, each painted by Eugene Richard with sprays of summer flowers scattered over a printed gilt net ground, 13.4 cm., printed crowned N mark, painted artist's initials, printed date code for 1855. **£100-150**

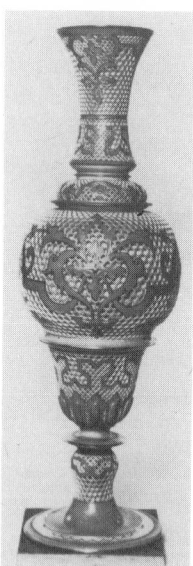

A Sèvres pierced and double walled vase, the body reticulated with stylised leaves, florets and strap-work, detailed in blue against honeycomb and geometric grounds outlined in pink and gilding, set on a square gilt-metal base, 55 cm., printed Louis Philippe monogram mark and date code for 1846. **£400-600**

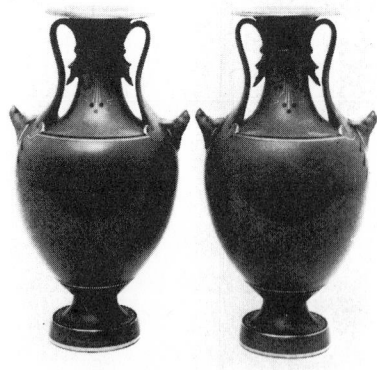

A pair of Sèvres vases, glazed in mushroom, the borders with blue and gilt stylised motifs, 31 cm., incised numerals, printed crowned N and date codes for 1868. **£150-250**

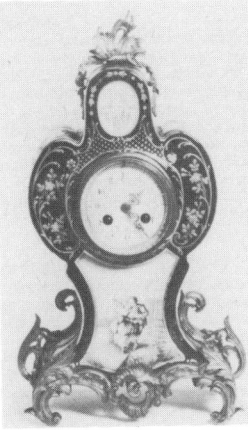

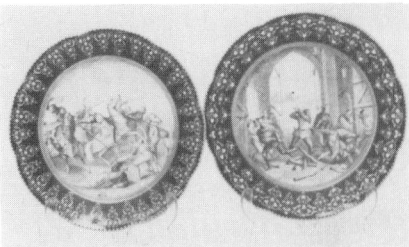

A 'Sèvres' clock case, painted by P. Roche, signed, with eighteenth century rustic lovers, the sides with floral sprays, on a bleu-de-roi ground with gilt foliate scrolls, mounted with a gilt metal foliate scroll, the movement stamped 'Vincent', 36 cm., late 19th C. **£350-500**

Two 'Sèvres' 'jewelled' plates, each painted with battle scenes, titled as 'Mort de Gaston de Foix, Bataille de Ravennes' and 'Prise du Chateau de Fougeray par Duguesdin', with a bleu-de-roi ground, rim gilt with scroll motifs and heightened in white, red and turquoise enamels, 24 cm., painted L's in blue, gilt titles, the porcelain late 18th C., the decoration mid 19th C. **£250-£350**

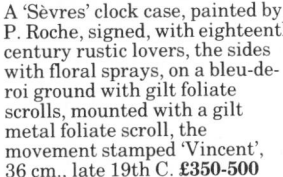

A 'Sèvres' casket, the gilt-metal hinged cover painted, and indistinctly signed, with a soldier giving a drink to an officer on horseback, probably intended as Napoleon, the base with landscape panels, all within ornate gilt borders on a bleu-de-roi ground, 34.5 cm., painted 'M:Imple. de Sèvres', late 19th C. **£350-500**

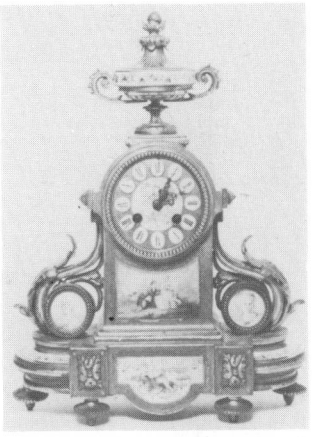

A 'Sèvres' gilt-bronze mounted clock case, with a bleu-céleste ground and gilt enrichment, 38 cm., the dial indistinctly signed, mid 19th C., on a gilt wood stand. **£300-350**

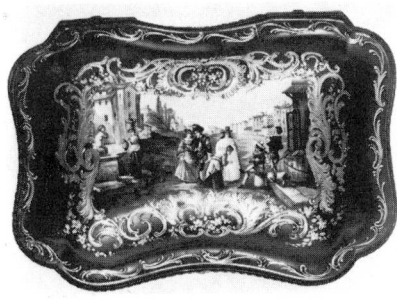

A 'Sèvres' casket, the metal mounted hinged cover painted with a street scene within gilt scrolls, the sides with landscape vignettes, all reserved on a ruby-red ground, the interior with floral sprays, 32.5 cm., painted interlaced L's, late 19th C. **£350-£450**

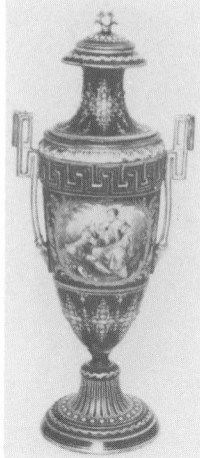

A 'Sèvres' 'jewelled' vase and cover, painted with panels of eighteenth century lovers in gardens and fruits and flowers, within tooled gilt borders on a bleu-de-roi ground, further enriched with gilt and polychrome enamel motifs, 34 cm., painted interlaced L's, mid 19th C. **£300-400**

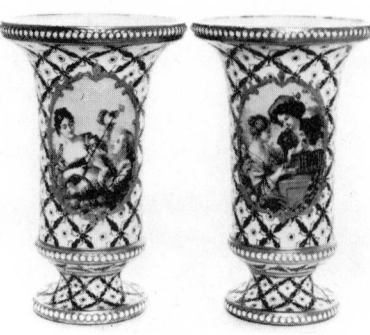

A pair of 'Sèvres' vases, each painted by Darty, signed, with a panel of rustic lovers and a riverscape, reserved on a trellis pattern ground of foliate motifs in blue, red, green and gilding, beaded borders, 23.5 cm., painted interlaced L's, c. 1900. **£200-300**

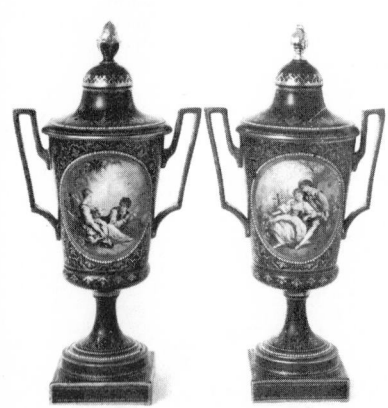

A pair of 'Sèvres' jewelled vases and covers, painted with panels of summer flowers and courting couples within floral gilt borders on a deep blue ground, bordered with mother-of-pearl jewelling, some wear, handles and one finial restored, 34 cm., painted interlaced L's, late 19th C. **£300-£400**

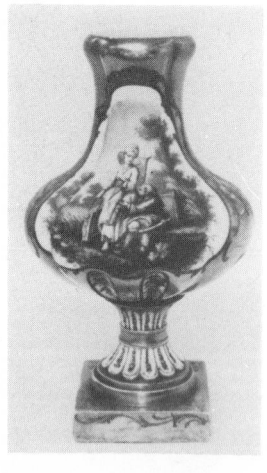

A pair of 'Sèvres' vases, each painted by Bertren, signed, with Chinoiserie panels of figures on a gilt ground scattered with sprays of flowers, one chipped, gilding rubbed, 36 and 36.8 cm., painted interlaced L's, mid 19th C. **£200-300**

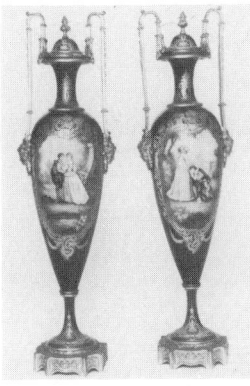

A pair of 'Sèvres' gilt metal mounted vases and covers, each painted by L. Bertren, signed, with eighteenth century lovers courting in gardens, the reverse with a riverscape, within gilt borders on a bleu-de-roi ground, small chip, 65 cm., painted interlaced L's, pseudo printed chateau mark, late 19th C. **£500-£700**

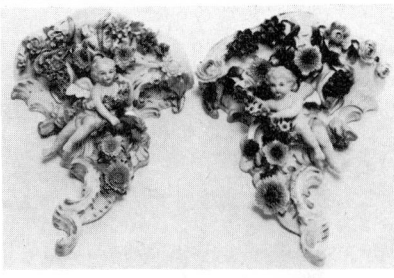

A set of four Sitzendorf wall brackets, moulded with scrolls and applied with a cherub amongst trails of flowers and foliage, chips, 20 cm., crossed parallel lines in underglaze-blue, c. 1900. **£250-350**

Make the most of Millers...

Remember that this book is a price *guide*, not a price *list*. Valuations given throughout apply to the specific prices shown and, though they may reasonably be taken as a guide to the values of other similar articles, other factors may also apply.
Condition of any article is of the utmost importance and must always be taken into account when negotiating the sale of any antique.

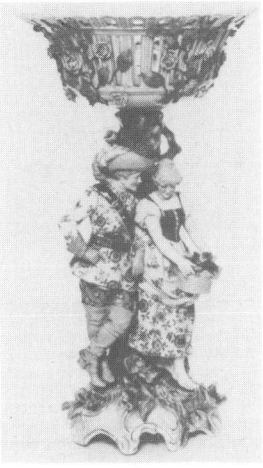

A Sitzendorf centrepiece, with pierced flared circular bowl, coloured and with gilt details, 54.5 cm., crossed parallel lines in underglaze-blue, late 19th C. **£250-300**

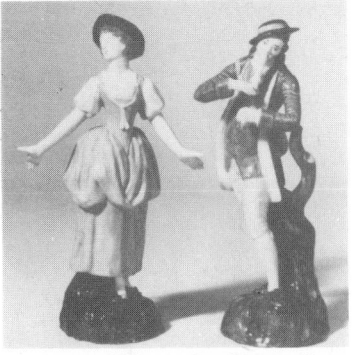

A pair of Thuringian figures of a young man and his companion, in black, green, iron-red, yellow, blue and pink, chip to his tree, she restored, c. 1770, probably Limbach, 20.5 cm. high. **£250-£350**

TOURNAI

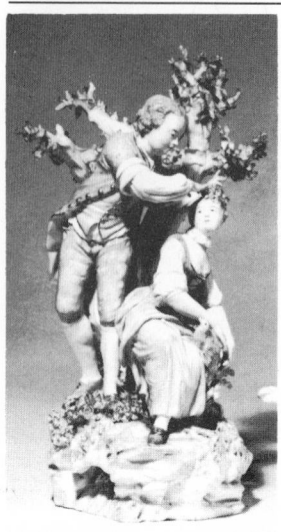

- founded in 1751 by F. J. Peterinck
- produced soft-paste porcelain
- early body tends to be a little greyish becoming more yellow later
- early wares were imitations of Meissen, then in the 1760's, copied Sèvres
- much porcelain sold 'in the white' and decorated elsewhere
- as with many other European factories, the Louis XVI style was followed in the 1780's
- amalgamated with the Saint-Amand-les-Eaux factory
- closed in the mid 19th C.

A Tournai polychrome group of a gallant and companion (L'adolescence), decorated in pastel colours, minor chips to extremities, c. 1760, 27 cm. high. **£1,000-1,500**
From a series depicting the Four Ages of Man.

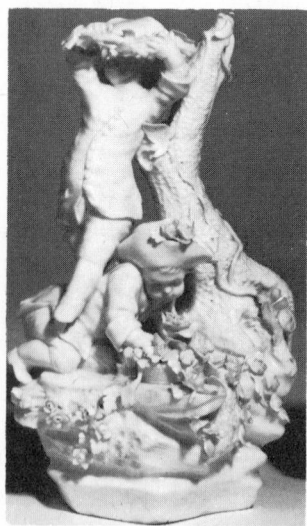

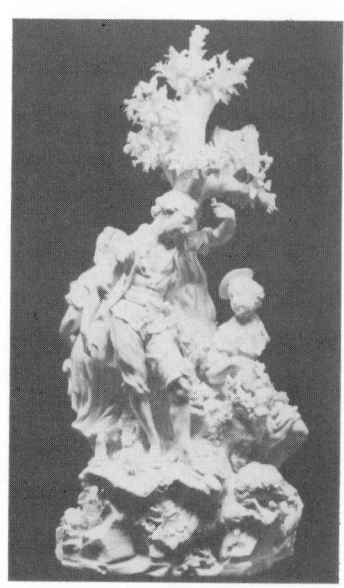

A very fine Tournai white group (Les Pêcheurs et Les Jardiniers), of four figures around a tree, emblematic of Earth and Water, one side with a seated youth putting fish into the apron of a girl in décolleté dress, the other with seated girl looking up at a standing youth, a net hanging in a delicately moulded tree, c. 1765, 35 cm. high. **£1,500-£2,000**

A Tournai white group of two boys collecting flowers, minor chips, c. 1770, 18.5 cm. high. **£300-400**

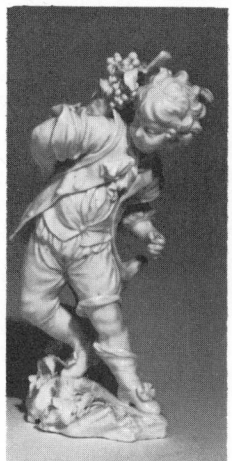
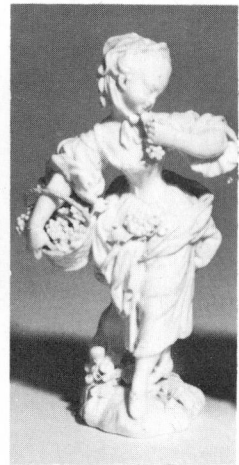

A pair of Tournai white figures
of a young boy and companion
modelled as vintagers, the
handle of her basket restored,
minor chips, c. 1770, 14 cm. high.
£500-600
*Tournai produced a large
number of figures in the white.*

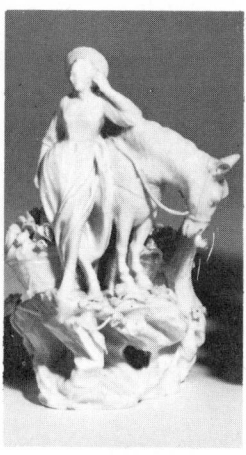
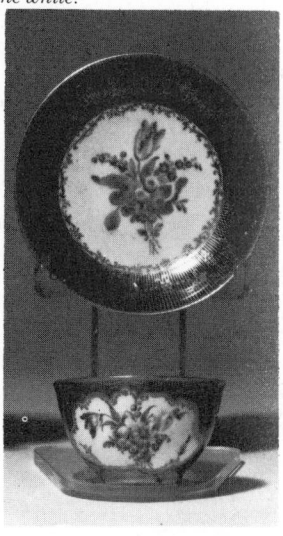

A Tournai white group of a
young woman with a pack-horse
and baskets of vegetables, ears of
horse restored, minor chips,
c. 1765, 13 cm. high. **£500-600**

A Venice (Cozzi) teabowl and
saucer, painted with panels of
flowers in shaped cartouches on
blue grounds, gilt with vertical
lines and swags of flowers, iron-
red anchor mark, c. 1770. **£200-
£300**
*Directly copied from Sèvres
originals.*

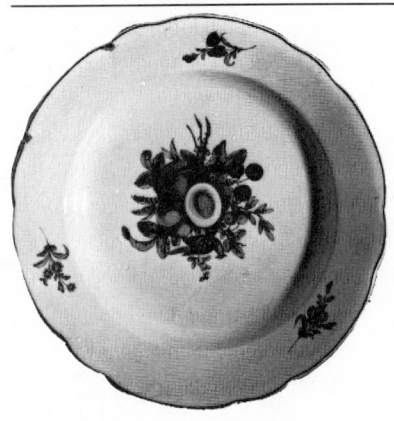

A Tournai soup plate, painted in the manner of Fidelle Duvivier, with a bird perched on a fruit, the rim with three flower sprays, glaze crack, incised P mark, c. 1765, 24 cm. diam. **£300-400**

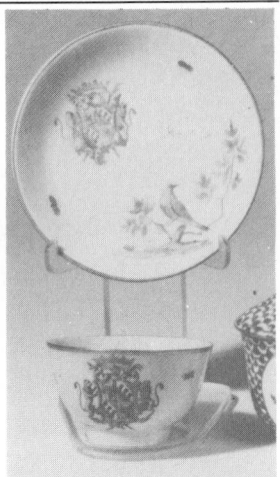

A pair of Venice (Cozzi) armorial saucers, from the Semitecoli service with Le Nove teabowls made to match, one teabowl cracked and chipped, the saucers with red anchor marks, one teabowl with star mark, 1735-80. **£700-900**

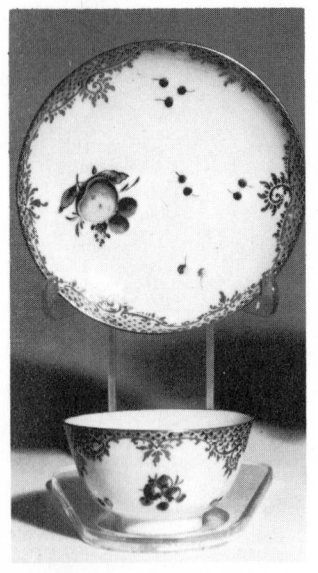

A pair of Venice (Cozzi) puce scale teabowls and saucers, painted with bunches of fruit, edged with gilt, red anchor marks, c. 1770. **£800-1,200** *'Puce scale' was directly copied from Meissen originals.*

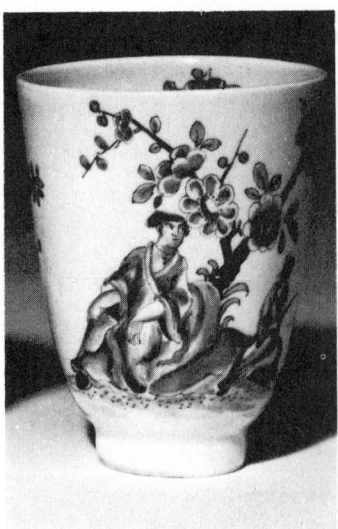

A Vienna early Du Paquier Chinoiserie beaker, painted with figures fishing and ducks beside a pagoda building in a river landscape, c. 1725. **£700-1,000**

VIENNA

- **factory founded by C. I. du Paquier in 1719 with the help of Stolzel and Hunger from Meissen**
- **the body of du Paquier wares has a distinctive smoky tone**
- **decoration tends to cover much of the body and is more elaborate than Meissen**
- **the 'State' period of the factory ran from 1744-84**
- **the style of this period was baroque, with scrollwork and lattice-like gilding**
- **plain bases were used from mid 1760's**
- **excellent figure modelling was undertaken by J. J. Niedermayer from 1747-84**
- **Konrad von Sorgenthal became director from 1784-1804**
- **the style became far less based on rococo and much simpler in taste, but with good strong colours and raised gilding**
- **factory closed in 1864**

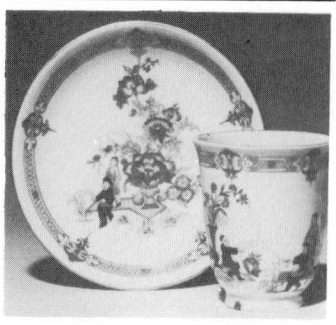

A Vienna Du Paquier beaker and saucer, painted in colours with Chinoiserie figures seated on terraces, birds and plants, the borders with iron-red trellis pattern panels divided by gilt scrolls, with gilt rims, c. 1745, saucer cracked. **£1,000-1,200**

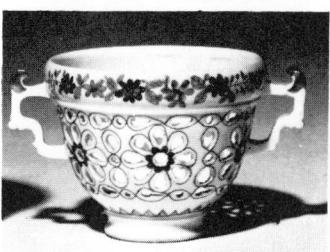

A Vienna Du Paquier pierced cup, painted in colours with flowerheads and foliage, the handles enriched in gilding, c. 1745, 9.5 cm. wide. **£1,000-£1,500**

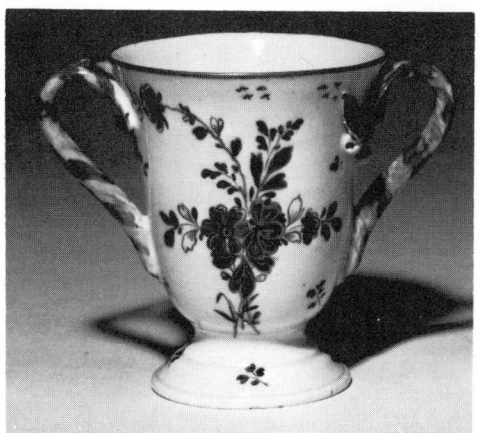

A Venice (Cozzi) beaker vase, painted with sprays of flowers in iron-red, blue and gilt, 1 cm. hair crack in rim, c. 1770, 10 cm. high. **£300-400**

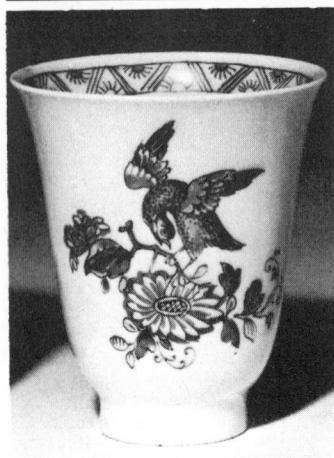

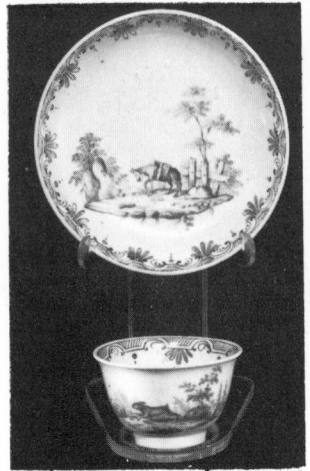

A Vienna Du Paquier armorial beaker, painted with a quarterly coat-of-arms with helmet, coronet, crest and foliage mantling, all en camaieu rose, the reverse painted in colours and gilt, c. 1730. **£700-1,000**

A Vienna Du Paquier saucer and a Vienna teabowl, painted en grisaille and gold with a pack-horse, a hare in landscape vignettes, the saucer with black beehive mark, the teabowl with blue beehive mark, 1742-45. **£300-400**

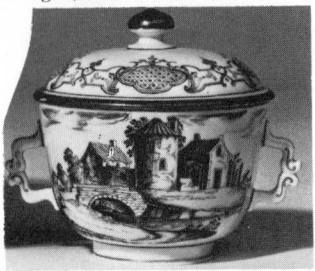

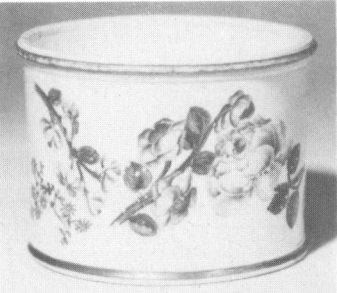

A Vienna Du Paquier cup and cover, painted in Schwarzlot with figures and rural buildings and a bridge over a river, the rims silvered, c. 1730, 11.5 cm. wide. **£2,500-3,000**

A Vienna Du Paquier cache pot, painted with Holzschnitt Blumen in bright colours between bands of gilding, c. 1740, 9.5 cm. high. **£600-800**
Note the crispness of the brushwork and the clarity of the enamels.

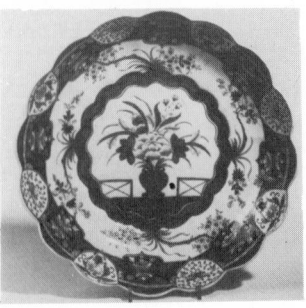

A large Vienna Du Paquier saucer dish, painted in the Imari style in iron-red, blue and gold, the reverse with eight lappets in iron-red edged in blue, c. 1730, 39.5 cm. diam. **£7,000-9,000**
An outstandingly successful example of the interpretation of Imari porcelain at the Du Paquier factory. Even at Meissen at this date, few dishes were fired of this size with any success.

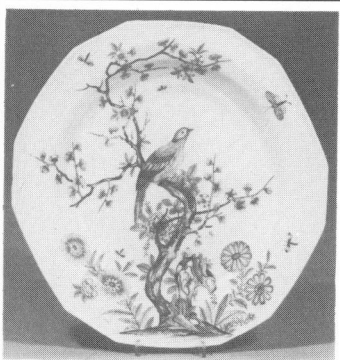

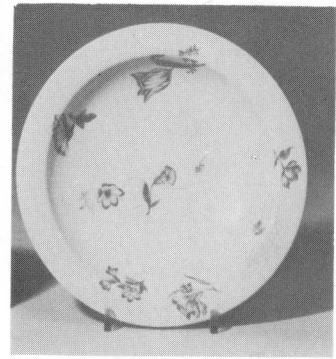

A Vienna Du Paquier large polygonal dish, painted in the Oriental style with a brightly plumaged bird perched on a flowering prunus, drilled in the centre and restored, rim chipped, c. 1735, 39.5 cm. diam. **£2,500-£3,500**

A Vienna Du Paquier saucer dish, painted with carefully drawn single flowers in colours, rim chip repair, c. 1735-40, 21.5 cm. diam. **£400-500**

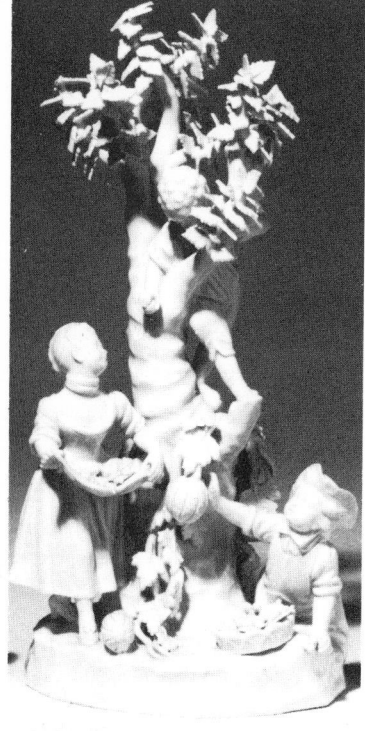

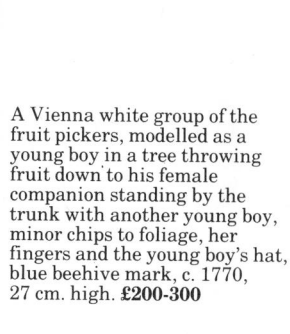

A Vienna group of an old man and a young girl, in black, green, pink, blue and yellow, impressed beehive mark, painter's mark ZO under the base, c. 1765, repair to his head and body, 13 cm. high. **£400-600**

A Vienna white group of the fruit pickers, modelled as a young boy in a tree throwing fruit down to his female companion standing by the trunk with another young boy, minor chips to foliage, her fingers and the young boy's hat, blue beehive mark, c. 1770, 27 cm. high. **£200-300**

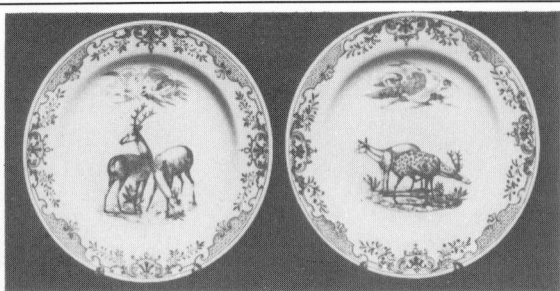

A pair of Vienna Du Paquier plates, from the Trivulzio service, painted perhaps by Jacob Helchis in Schwarzlot and gold with a spotted deer and hind, the borders with Laub-und-Bandelwerk and Gitterwerk panels, c. 1740, 25 cm. diam. **£3,000-3,500**

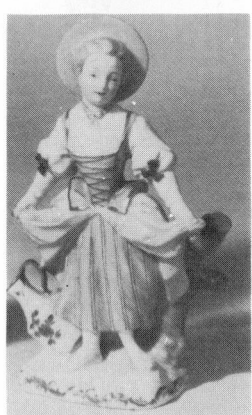

A Vienna figure of a young girl, in pink, green, yellow and orange, restoration to pitcher and the tip of her hands, blue beehive mark, c. 1760, 16 cm. high. **£500-700**

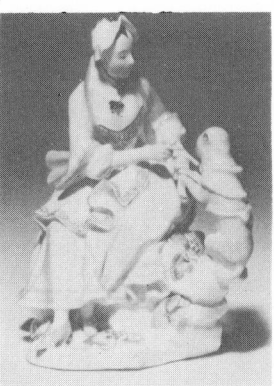

A Vienna group of a young woman, minute chips, impressed E marks, c. 1775, 14.5 cm. high. **£650-750**

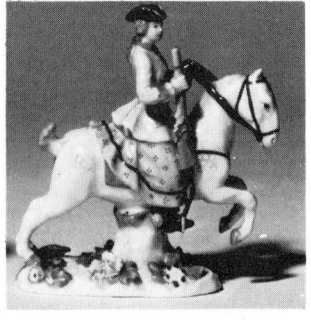

A Vienna equestrian figure of a sportswoman in black, blue, yellow and puce, blue beehive mark, c. 1775, minor chips to horse's ears and foliage, 9 cm. high. **£500-600**

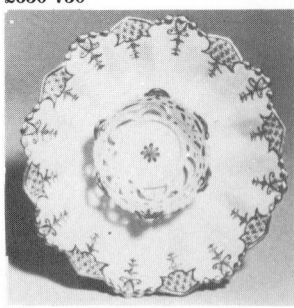

A Vienna Du Paquier trembleuse saucer, painted in red, green, puce and blue, with gilt rim, minor rim chip, moulded mock Chinese seal mark, c. 1725. **£1,300-1,600**

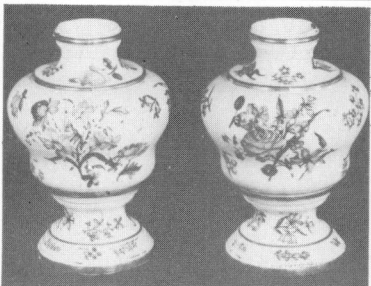

A pair of Vienna Du Paquier vases, painted with Holzschnitt Blumen and with four gilt bands, slight chips to one foot, c. 1735, 13 cm. high. **£1,600-2,000**

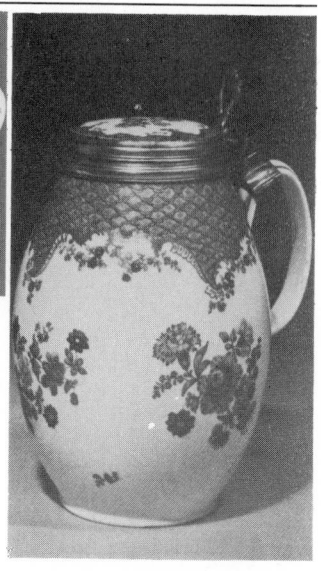

A Vienna barrel-shaped tankard, painted in colours with bouquets and sprays of flowers within puce scale pattern borders, enriched with gilding, the metal gilt rim with hinged mount, 20 cm. high, impressed W, 2 marks, for 1777. **£500-600** *Design is copied from a 'Compagnie des Indes' original.*

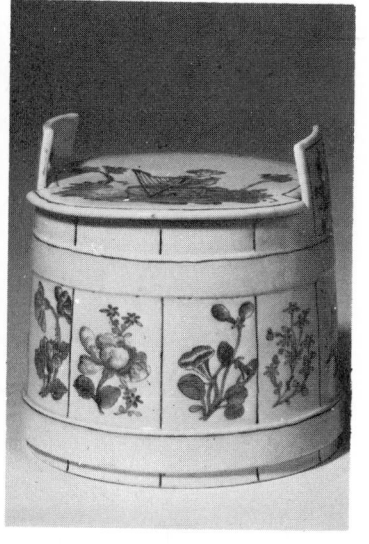

A Vienna Du Paquier butter tub and cover, formed as a half barrel, one handle restored and one corner of the cover, c. 1740, 12.5 cm. diam. **£3,000-5,000** *Du Paquier is noted for its somewhat academic style of botanical painting.*

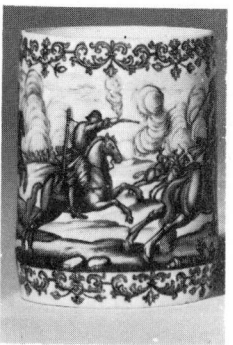

A Vienna Du Paquier Hausmalerei cylindrical mug, painted in Schwarzlot in the Preissler workshop with a military encounter, with traces of gilding, foot rim chip repair, c. 1730, 9.5 cm. high. **£4,000-£6,000**

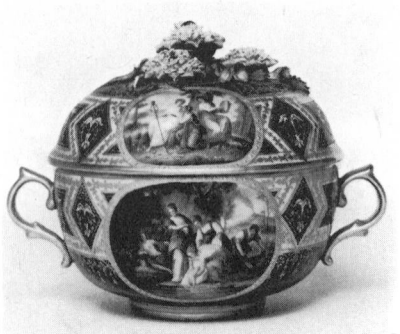

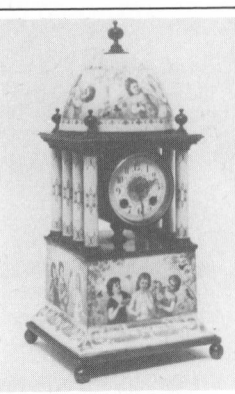

A 'Vienna' bowl and cover, each piece painted with panels of mythological subjects, named on the reverse, reserved on a deep lilac ground with pale blue and gilt borders, 18 cm. over handles, shield in underglaze-blue, painted titles, late 19th C. **£150-250**

A 'Vienna' gilt metal mounted clock case, painted by Ullman, signed, between gilt borders on a pale pink ground, 39.5 cm., shield in underglaze-blue, late 19th C. **£800-1,200**

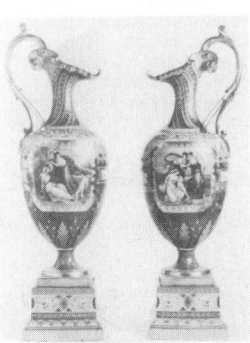

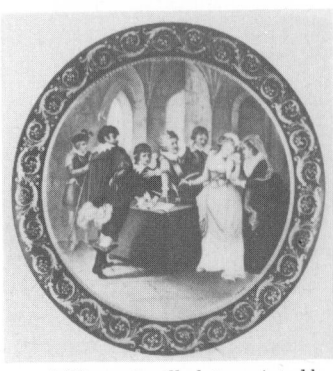

A pair of 'Vienna' ewers and stands, painted with panels of mythological subjects on a blue and ruby red ground with gilt borders and polychrome panels, stems chipped, 57 cm., shield in underglaze-blue, mid 19th C. **£700-900**

A 'Vienna' wall plate, painted by O. Drefset, signed, with a distraught Mary, Queen of Scots, forced to sign the document renouncing her succession rights, within a gilt scrolled ruby red ground border, 41.6 cm., shield in underglaze-blue, painted title, late 19th C. **£500-£600**

A large 'Vienna' plaque, painted by Otto Dressl, signed, with a panel of 'Fortune', reserved on a deep lilac ground with gilt foliate scroll motifs and a pale blue raised rim, 48.5 cm., cancelled impressed factory mark, painted shield and title, c. 1800. **£450-650**

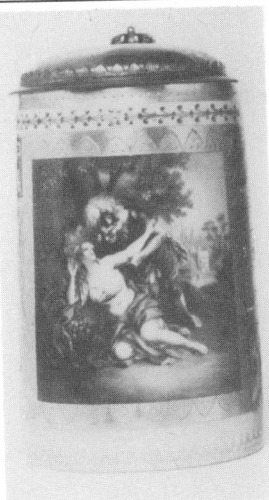

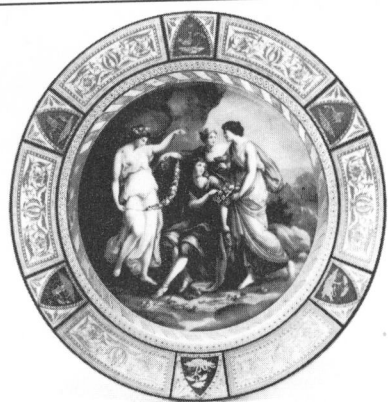

A 'Vienna' plate painted with a mythological scene of Telemachus, within a polychrome border with gilt foliate scrolls, vignettes and borders, 24.5 cm., shield in underglaze-blue, printed title, late 19th C. **£200-250**

A 'Vienna' gilt metal mounted tankard, painted with a panel of 'The Rape of the Sabine', on a polychrome ground with formal gilt borders, 16 cm., shield in underglaze-blue, painted title, late 19th C. **£250-350**

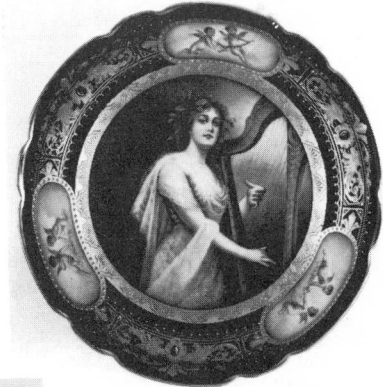

A 'Vienna' fruit stand, painted by Fritsch, signed, with 'Solace in Music', reserved on a royal blue ground with gilt borders flanking panels of putti and gilt rustic vignettes, 23 cm., painted shield and title, late 19th C. **£150-200**

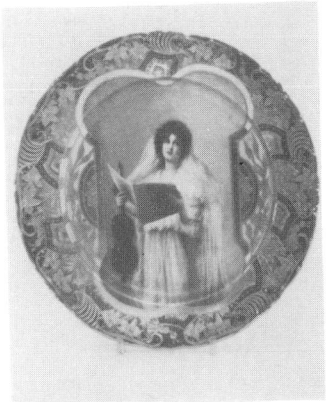

A 'Vienna' wall plate, painted by Wagner, signed, with 'Abendlied', within a shaded blue rim, gilt with flowers and scrolls, 30.4 cm., painted shield and title, c. 1900. **£200-300**

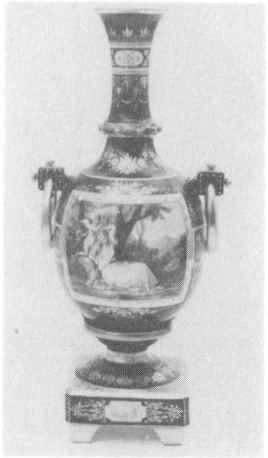

A 'Vienna' vase, in two sections, the almost spherical body painted with two allegorical panels of love, on a ruby red ground, the knopped neck with similar panels, set on a matching square base, base with hair crack, 51 cm., painted shield and titles, c. 1900. **£300-400**

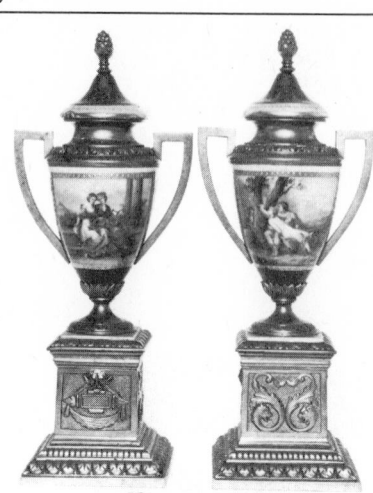

A pair of gilt metal mounted 'Vienna' vases and covers, painted by Neuman, signed, with a mythological panel on a polychrome and gilt panelled ground, covers damaged, 24 cm., c. 1900. **£150-250**

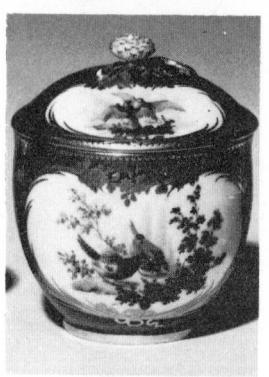

A Vincennes bleu céleste sugar bowl and cover, painted with brightly coloured birds, within gilt foliate cartouches, finial repaired, blue interlaced L marks enclosing the date letter for 1754, 19.5 cm. high. **£200-£300**

A pair of 'Vienna' vases of 'Chastity' and 'Flower of Youth', each painted by Wagner, signed, cracks restored, 25.5 cm., painted shield, title, 4451 DN, late 19th C. **£300-400**

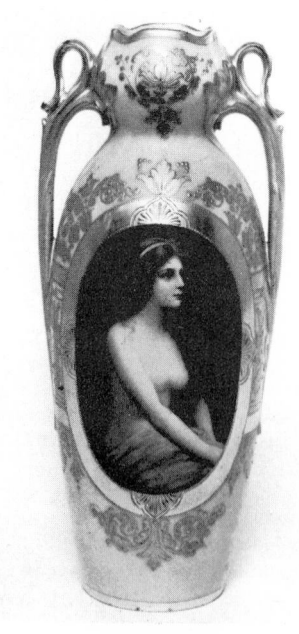

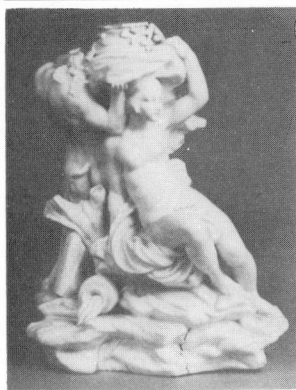

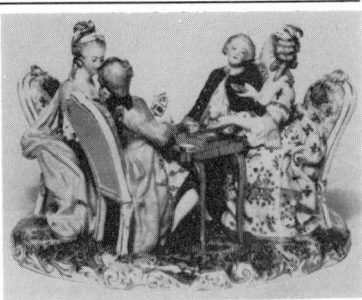

A Volkstedt (Eckert & Co.) group of card players, the whole coloured with pastel shades with gilt details and raised on a 'carpeted' moulded gilt-scroll base, 27 cm., underglaze-blue, crossed swords and EC, late 19th C. **£300-400**

A Vincennes white group of Naiad and a satyr, minor chips, satyr's left arm originally missing, c. 1750, 23 cm. high. **£300-400**. If perfect: **£700-900**
It has been suggested that this group is part of four and symbolic of the Four Great Rivers of France, Rhône, Rhine, Seine and Loire.

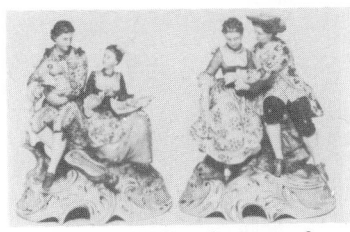

A pair of Volkstedt groups of lovers, 21.5 and 22 cm., hayfork marks in blue, late 19th C. **£200-£230**

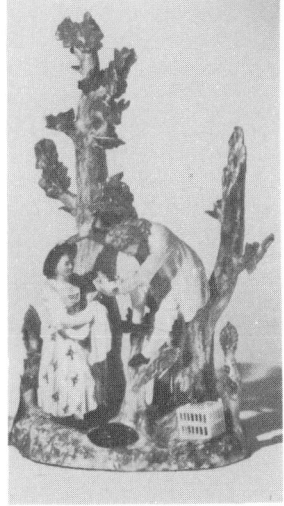

A Wallendorf bird's nest group, of a youth and a girl, their clothes in buff yellow, pink, the tree is in russet, green and turquoise, on rockwork base, chips to leaves, c. 1775, 28 cm. high. **£1,000-1,400**

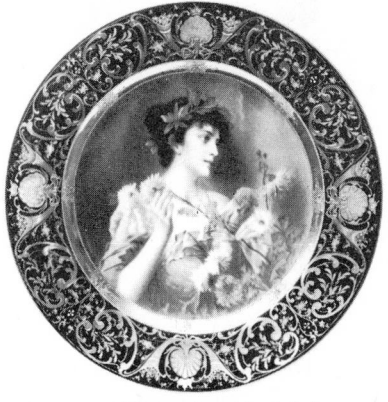

A Volkstedt cabinet plate, painted by Stoch, signed, with 'Chrysanthemum', within a royal blue ground rim, gilt with foliate scrolls, shell motifs and flowers, 24 cm., crossed pitchforks, gilt obliterated mark and title. c. 1900. **£300-400**

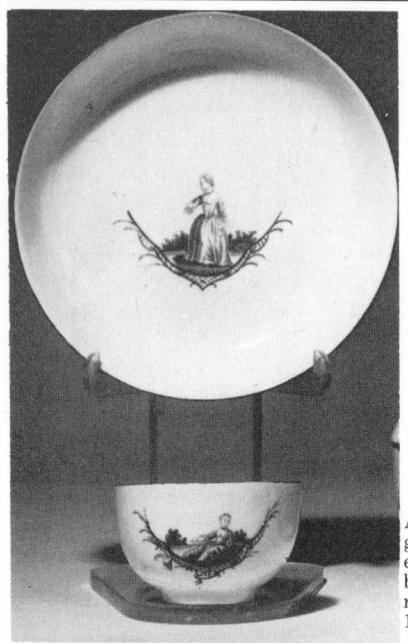

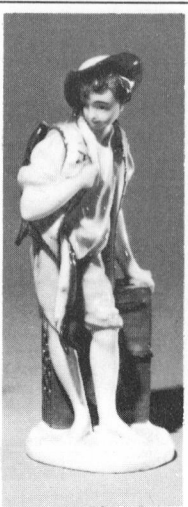

A Zürich figure of a fisherboy, in green lined yellow hat, his jerkin edged in iron-red with buff breeches, white circular base, restored, incised K3, c. 1780, 13.5 cm. high. **£1,000-1,200**

A pair of Weesp teabowls and saucers, painted with ladies and a gentleman in landscapes within open purple rococo cartouches, chocolate rims, one teabowl chipped, the saucers with blue crossed swords marks and three dots, 1765-70. **£1,000-£1,600**

A Zürich bowl, painted with two landscape vignettes, the larger with five figures on shore and three in a boat, the smaller with three figures in river and lake landscapes, the rim gilt, blue Z mark, c. 1770, 18 cm. diam. **£1,000-1,400**

ZURICH

- **factory founded in 1763 by A. Spengler who had come from Höchst**
- **began by making soft-paste porcelain**
- **by c. 1765 making hard-paste**
- **with clear glaze**
- **made a great deal of underglaze-blue wares**
- **styles and designs mainly copied from Meissen**
- **many fine Swiss landscapes painted**
- **factory closed in 1790**

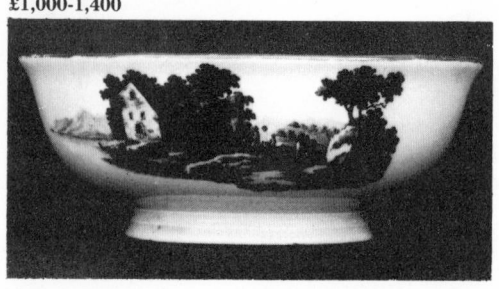

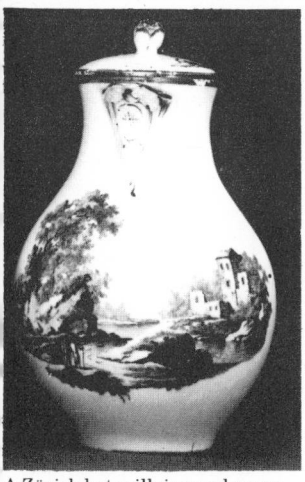

A Zürich hot milk jug and cover, painted with two figures in a river landscape, crack in the body, blue Z and two dots mark, c. 1700, 16 cm. high. **£250-350**

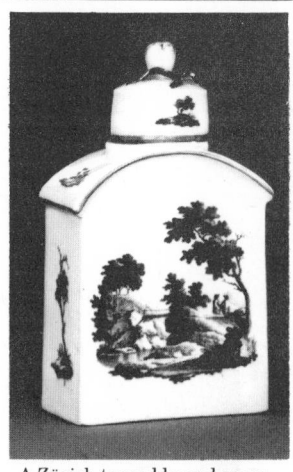

A Zürich teacaddy and cover, painted with figures in landscapes, small chip to shoulder, blue Z and dots mark, ID incised, c. 1775, 13.5 cm. high. **£1,500-2,000**

Right
A Zürich baluster sugar-caster, finial lacking, blue Z mark, c. 1800, 18 cm. high. **£450-£550**

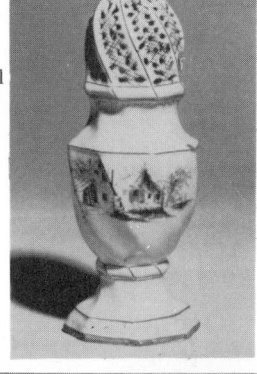

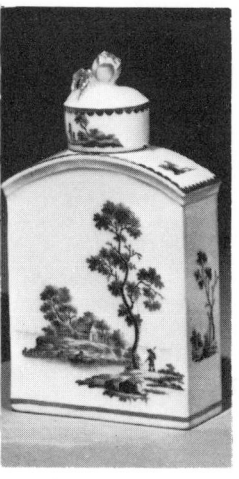

A Zürich teacaddy and cover, painted with a fisherman and figures, the sides, shoulders and cover with lesser vignettes of trees, c. 1770, 14 cm. high. **£1,100-1,500**

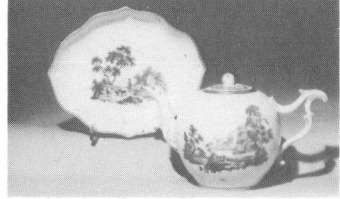

A Zürich teapot, cover and stand, painted with peasant figures in landscapes vignettes and with gilt dentil rims, minute chip to cover, the teapot with blue Z and dots mark, the stand with Z only, c. 1770, the teapot 21 cm. wide. **£2,200-2,500**

117

INDEX